Welcome to Islam

Welcome to Islam

A Convert's Tale

Lucy Bushill-Matthews

continuum

Continuum
The Tower Building
11 York Road
London SE1 7NX

80 Maiden Lane
Suite 704
New York, NY 10038

www.continuumbooks.com

© Lucy Bushill-Matthews 2008

The Message of the Qu'ran, translated and explained by Muhammad Asad © 2003 by kind permission of The Book Foundation.

'African Christmas' by Ed Jordan from *African Christmas* © 1998 by kind permission of Universal.

British Library Cataloguing-in-Publication Data
A catalogue record for this book is available from the British Library.

ISBN-10: PB: 1-8470-6216-4
ISBN-13: PB: 978-1-8470-6216-1

Library of Congress Cataloguing-in-Publication Data
A catalog record for this book is available from the Library of Congress.

Bushill-Matthews, Lucy.
  Welcome to Islam : tales of a convert / Lucy Bushill-Matthews.
    p. cm.
  Includes bibliographical references.
  ISBN 978-1-84706-216-1
  1. Bushill-Matthews, Lucy. 2. Muslim converts from
Christianity–Great Britain–Biography. 3. Islam–Great Britain. I.
Title.

  BP170.5.B87 2008
  297.092–dc22
  [B]

                                                                    2008001169

Typeset by BookEns Ltd, Royston, Herts.
Printed and bound in Great Britain by Ashford Colour Press Ltd, Gosport, Hampshire.

This book is dedicated to my parents,
in whose footsteps I am attempting to follow,
albeit in my own way.

Contents

Acknowledgements

Thank you to God, the Most Kind, the Most Merciful, who knew how events would unfold before I did.

Thank you to my husband, for remaining a voice of reason throughout life's chaos and for coming up with the title of the book. Thank you for eventually reading it, even if it was just days before it went to be published.

Thank you to my three children, for being you. One day you each might read this and learn how impetuous I was as a young student. Please don't get any ideas.

Thank you to my neighbours, my friends and my family who have all agreed to be mentioned - particularly my parents. I know you will be very careful what you say to me in future in case I decide to write about it.

Thank you to Heana for inspiring me to write in the first place. Thank you to those who have read and commented on parts of the book, in England and in South Africa - Nasheeba, Fozia, Rizia, Dana, Maureen, Nina, Kirsten as well as my family. And to those of you who intended to comment but never quite got around to it: well, I appreciate the intention.

Thank you to Rebecca at Continuum, for having faith in me. Thank you to the organization Islam is Peace (www.islamispeace.org.uk), for letting me use your material both in the glossary and on my fledgling website (www.lucybushillmatthews.com).

Thank you to my Austrian friend Fatima and Irish friend Batool -

you have both been invaluable sources of wisdom and advice for many years.

And to my dear English friends Wendy and Lena - much of this could be your story too.

Introduction

The taxi driver picked me up from my office for a five-minute journey. 'What's it like being oppressed?' he asked, eyeing my scarf. I briefly considered telling him I thought it was probably more fun than being a taxi driver but I didn't really want to get confrontational – and anyway one in seven Pakistani men in the UK are taxi drivers as well as being Muslim.[1] So I just explained that I wasn't oppressed, was Muslim of my own free will, and was actually fairly happy with my life. I could tell he wasn't convinced.

Muslims feature in the news as a headline item almost daily now, yet many of us have picked up only a little information about Islam along the way. In a YouGov survey a few years ago, two-thirds of respondents said they obtained what information they did have from television and newspapers.[2] When they were asked: 'How much do you feel you know about Britain's Muslim community?' 60 per cent thought they didn't know very much and another 10 per cent answered that they knew absolutely nothing. A number of people have asked me: 'Are you an Islam?' or 'Why are you taking time off at Christmas? It's not as if you believe in Jesus.' When the religious holiday approached, my neighbour Jane wished me 'Happy Diwali'.

;lam

...ch more about Islam and the Muslims, finding out
_ aith overall or going deeper into aspects of it like Muslim
,ayer, *Hajj*, women, conversion, extremism, parenting, politics,
history ... but real life isn't quite like the textbooks.

Praying is described in guides to Islam as an opportunity five
times a day to focus directly and humbly on God. And indeed it is.
But no one mentions how hard it is to focus when you have one
child climbing on your back every time you prostrate on the floor –
and another screaming 'I've finished' from the vicinity of the
bathroom.

Then there is the mosque, a place of prayer and a community
centre. One Ramadan, I dropped in to my local mosque a few
minutes after sunset to break the fast and to start eating. I was with
my non-fasting four year old, still twirling around in her ballet tutu. A
plethora of male mosque 'elders' attended to our every need, racing
to serve food to us. One has to tread carefully in a mosque though:
when coordinating a children's *madrasa*, or Islamic school, performance about God's creation, for parents at the very same mosque, I
allowed one three-year-old boy to wear face paint to look like a dog.
I became a social outcast among most of the local Muslim
community for months due to violating the custom of not allowing
dogs into a mosque – a tradition that they were now extending to
include face-painted dog whiskers.

The differences in Islamic practice became a bit clearer to me
when I attended a talk at the Islamic Foundation in Leicester. The
speaker described Islam as 'a forty-lane highway'. What one Muslim
finds *halal*, or acceptable, can be decreed *haram*, or forbidden, by
another. Since then, I have met many Muslims who are in very
different lanes.

Meet a Muslim

We might not have the time or the inclination to r
Islam. We are often too exhausted by life or have rather more
pressing things to do like preparing for work and/or ironing the
school uniform for tomorrow. Wouldn't it be so much easier if you
could just chat with someone about real-life incidents relating to
their faith? But you may not have the opportunity: almost 60 per
cent of people in the USA have never even met a Muslim.[3]

In the UK, the opportunities for interaction between Muslims
and everyone else are increasing. More than half of UK Muslims
are born in Britain. Muslims now make up around 2 million or
nearly 3 per cent of the population in England and Wales. In
London, one person in seven is Muslim. When I became Muslim in
the early 1990s my father was understandably concerned that, by
becoming Muslim, I might end up in a segregated 'ghetto'. He
needn't have worried. The 2001 census shows that the most
segregated religious groups geographically are the Jews and
Sikhs.[4] Separate research has shown, unsurprisingly, that the
people most isolated from meeting people in other ethnic groups
are in fact the ethnic majority group:[5] the Christians, followed by
people of no religion. At the time, I assured my father I would be
fine: I don't think I would have been very popular if I had
responded by suggesting that, statistically at least, he was the
more isolated one.

Wind chimes and the weather

Many British people have still never set foot in a Muslim home. Ben
fell into that category. He was a student friend of Gehane, a relative
who was staying with us. He came by to pick her up one Sunday
afternoon – and we could see the amusement on Ben's face as he
witnessed the chaotic scene. My husband was absorbed in watching

the television, where cars were zooming repeatedly around a race track; I was attempting to make wind chimes with our three children aged at the time between two and six, from one of those kits that were meant to be incredibly easy to use but never turned out that way. This process involved mixing and painting plaster and strategically dangling bits from each other and was a big mess with broken plaster everywhere. Ben told Gehane he didn't expect Muslim families to be making wind chimes. He confessed he had half-expected us to be making bombs. Ben even wanted to come around again – or perhaps it was just to check that we remained 'normal' the second time he visited.

I have been into schools and other organizations and have talked with adults and children about Islam and Muslims – and have had some wonderful and some disheartening experiences. One of the most poignant questions I was asked after a talk was: 'What is the weather like in their world?' This question came from a child with at least five Muslim schoolmates, all of whom lived within a few kilometres of the school.

Like all Muslims, I share the same world as this child – and the same weather. We are all strongly affected by both national and global events, including a flurry of media reporting of Muslim-related issues. I was once interviewed by the *Sun* newspaper for a feature article on Islam and converts, but the piece was quickly ditched in favour of a breaking story headed: 'The Taliban removed my nail varnish'.

Structure of the book

This book takes a look at real life inside – and outside – a Muslim home. It starts with my conversion to Islam, as both Muslims and non-Muslims are often vaguely interested in – and, more usually, perplexed about – why anyone would undertake such a step. The book then moves on to what it is like to live daily life as a Muslim:

getting married; going on holiday; at work; making a pilgrimage to Mecca; bringing up children; experiencing both Christmas time and *Eid* in England; and living within a broad local community of English people, Muslims, and people who are comfortable with being both.

Each chapter starts with a quote from the Qur'an and with a *hadith* – a saying from Muhammad, whom Muslims believe to be a Prophet of God. Many people have heard of the Qur'an but have little idea what might be in it; and Muslims believe that we should do our best to follow what Muhammad said and did. Faith-based issues behind the anecdotes are explained in context in a straightforward way – like who or what Allah is, why some Muslim women wear a scarf and what Muslim children are really learning when they go to a *madrasa*.

For those who want to know more, detailed information for each chapter is provided at the end of the book.

Note that the English names for the Prophets have been used throughout. For Muslims, it is a mark of respect to say 'peace be upon him' immediately after mentioning anyone whom Muslims believe to be a Prophet. However, this has not been followed in the book in order not to interrupt the flow. It is hoped that Muslims would say the greetings of peace as they read.

1 Embracing Faith

'And say: We believe in that which has been bestowed from on high upon us, as well as that which has been bestowed upon you: or our God and your God is one and the same, and it is unto Him that We [all] surrender ourselves.'

(Qur'an 29:46)

'I am most akin to Jesus Christ among the whole of mankind. All the Prophets are of different mothers but belong to one religion. No Prophet was raised between me and Jesus.'[1]

(Saying of Muhammad)

Renée made a special effort with dinner and served up the largest pork cutlets I had ever seen. My heart sank.

I was 19 years old and in the middle of my first year at university. My parents had invited me to join them on a short break to visit my sister Julie, who was studying at a university near Amsterdam. I had spent the ferry journey teaching my other sibling, my eight-year-old brother William, how to do ballet. Just before we docked in Holland, William proudly showed off his new-found skills to our parents. It was a happy occasion. We were together as a family for the first time in many months.

We were staying with Dutch friends Renée and Theo, whom my parents had known for years. How could I tell Renée I had given up pork three months ago? I hadn't told anyone in my family. I tucked in. And then Theo passed around the wine. Should I tell Theo I had

given that up too? William was drinking Coca-Cola; I asked him to
pass it to me. I thought no one would notice. But my father did.

Coming out

'I hear Muslims think Coca-Cola has some alcohol in it,' my father
commented. Why did he say that? I hadn't mentioned my developing
interest in Islam to anyone outside of my university. Perhaps it was just
a random remark. But I couldn't help blushing. My father noticed that
too. 'You are not one of them, are you?' he added. Everyone laughed
but my father continued to look at me. And my face went redder.

The light-hearted dinner-table conversation came to an abrupt
halt. I ended up 'confessing' that I was seriously interested in Islam.
My father remained calm and rational. 'Let's talk a bit more about this
some other time,' he said, evenly. My mother didn't say a word – she
looked visibly upset. Julie and Renée's daughter started discussing
the nightlife culture in the Netherlands – and I started hoping that
the previous little exchange might somehow be forgotten. After
dinner, I went off to help with the washing-up. The moment I
entered the kitchen Renée asked 'How could you do this do your
mother?'

I was not planning to tell my parents anything about my
investigations until I had made up my mind. And now I had to justify
my thought process – and I hadn't even decided anything yet. It was
all moving way too quickly. How could I have got myself into this
situation?

How could I? How could I even think about rejecting the way my
own father and mother had brought me up? They had spent so
many years providing so much: a stable environment, moral values,
endless collections from school, friends and after-school activities,
numerous birthday parties and outings and frequent childhood visits
to the Church-based Sunday school, where at Easter time I made
little crosses and stuffed moss into a model of Jesus's garden.

It wasn't personal, and it wasn't intentional – and anyway, I hadn't even made up my mind.

My first Muslim

The first Muslim I ever met was on my sixteenth birthday, in 1987, more than three years earlier. I had entered the mixed sixth form of a traditional English boarding school, to join the boys aged between sixteen and eighteen. Until then, I had been at an all-girls school in Surrey. I had never met anyone who wasn't Christian in one form or another. And everyone I had ever known was white, apart from the girl from whom I was inseparable when I was nine years old, my best friend Asha, whose parents came from India and who happened to be dark brown.

In the first week of term, I was getting lost all over my new school while trying to get to the different A-level maths classes. Without fail, I was late. Julian was the only person from my maths set who lived in the boys' boarding house where I had a study but he didn't seem to notice that I was turning up after each class had started. A girl from the year above was rather more perceptive and took me to the door of Julian's room to introduce us to see if he could help me find my way.

Julian was different from the other boys, despite the shared interests in music, competitive sport and gadgets. He was a British Muslim, half-Iranian and half-English. Our first conversation was centred on school fees: he worked out the total cost to his stepfather for himself and three brothers to go through five years of boarding school and explained how his stepfather had planned carefully to finance it all. The second time we met, we were engrossed in conversation, so I missed lunch. Julian, of course, missed lunch too, although it didn't seem to bother him. But I never ever missed a meal. I had just made a major sacrifice and Julian wasn't even aware of it.

Julian's attitude to alcohol was unusual. Most of the teenagers around us were focused at the weekends on getting 'trashed', drinking until they threw up; he had other interests that didn't involve being sick. He didn't even have a glass of wine when a few of us went out for a meal – even though I had always understood that drinking wine was a very grown-up thing to do. And as our conversations grew more wide ranging he began to challenge my thinking. Through school and church, I had been taught for years that Jesus was both the Son of God and also God in human form. I was happy with my life; I wasn't happy to be challenged. But he did help me with my maths.

Just a friend

My mother found out about Julian when I went home one weekend. I was in the kitchen, explaining to her and my sister what the school was like. 'So what's going on between you and this boy?' she asked as we washed and dried the dishes. 'Oh nothing, he's just a friend,' I told her. 'He's a good friend; he could never be anything else. Anyway, he's too short.' My sister seemed suspicious; I have no idea why.

I started to invite Julian home for Sunday lunch. My father established that Julian had some connection to Iran and interrogated him about his views on the Western hostages that some Iranians had taken. He expected this seventeen-year-old to have a coherent explanation. Julian had no idea about Iran and knew even less about any hostages. It was a short conversation.

Julian then stayed over for a week of the school holidays – my parents gave him a downstairs room well away from me. On a cold night, my mother kindly lent him a hot water bottle: she didn't know it had developed a leak but Julian soon found out as scalding water slowly seeped into his bed. They grew to like him, despite his lack of knowledge of international politics. And he grew to like them too, despite getting soaked.

When he went back to stay for the rest of the holidays with his family, who were expatriates in Kenya, we wrote to each other every night. My sister had been right to be suspicious.

Freedom of speech

In my second and final year of sixth form, in 1988, Salman Rushdie's fictional book *The Satanic Verses* was published. Through school, I had been awarded a book voucher, and used it to buy a copy. The bookseller stuck my certificate inside the novel and then wrapped it in a brown paper bag to keep my controversial purchase discreet. I had never read a book about Muslims before – fiction or non-fiction – and having to purchase one in a paper bag added to the novelty.

I knew by then that worshipping Allah – and only Allah – was central to Muslim belief. Muslims believed that Angel Gabriel, known in Arabic as Gibreel, revealed Allah's words to Muhammad. Salman Rushdie didn't specifically mention Muhammad himself – but he did write about a prophet named Mahound, an obscure insulting European name for Muhammad. The book clearly indicated that Mahound – or Muhammad – spoke verses that were revealed by an angel named Gibreel but who was nicknamed Satan. These verses encouraged the worship of idols and were inspired by the Devil rather than by God. Salman Rushdie's story didn't seem designed to win friends among his Muslim readership; in fact, it appeared gratuitously offensive.[2]

Salman Rushdie was given extensive media coverage – initially he said he wasn't Muslim, then he said he was, then he said he wasn't. I was confused; it sounded like he was too. The Muslims were unhappy with him whatever he said. Many Muslims seemed to have read it since I presumed no one would burn a book just based on hearsay. But I couldn't finish the book myself; I found it too strange and simply too boring.

I knew I was a Christian. I was not particularly a practising

Christian, given that I only went to church if my parents or the school made me. However, if ever I had a form to complete that asked a question about religion, I always put 'Church of England'. It certainly sounded like it was the right kind of religion for an English person.

Julian and I chose different ways to spend our 'gap year' before university. For the first four months, I wrote to him daily and included lots of questions about Islam to make sure he wrote back to me too. He always did.

A walk in the park

I spent those four months working in London, thanks to a scholarship that I had won in my last year at school. Late one evening after work, there was a dinner scheduled for all of us who had ever been awarded one of these, held at the private home of the lady providing the scholarship. She lived in London's Regent's Park. I thought it would be a good opportunity to make a quick visit to the Central Mosque before the dinner – I had never been to a mosque before and I knew both places were in the vicinity of that park.

My first discovery was that the mosque was not actually in Regent's Park – or at least it wasn't anywhere near the Underground station of that name. It hadn't occurred to me to check the London 'A-Z' before I left. I walked for ages, in the cold and dark, wrapped up in my winter coat and scarf. As I walked, I felt a growing sense of excitement combined with an element of fear of the unknown; and I wasn't even sure why I was going there or what I was hoping to find.

When I eventually arrived, a man noticed me at the entrance and – after gently explaining how we must all be modestly dressed inside a mosque and asking me to put my winter scarf over my head – he generously bought me a book from the mosque bookshop. It was called *What Everyone Should Know about Islam and Muslims*. He then spent the next half-hour standing just below me on the stairs leading to the downstairs halls, explaining his faith. I found out later that I had been fortunate: other women have been either ignored completely or besieged by men proposing instant marriage.

Before I left, I quickly looked into the prayer areas of the mosque: there was no furniture; only a wall-to-wall carpet and a few people were quietly reading; others were praying in silence.

Worlds apart

I then had to run for my dinner engagement. I was very late and it turned out to be a very smart place – they even had a photograph hanging above the toilet showing the family chatting to the Queen. The conversation at dinner centred on business and particularly acquisitions in the media industry. It felt a world away from my previous conversation. My upbringing had prepared me well for this dinner yet there seemed to be something missing. There had been an unmistakable and inexplicable attraction to the serene open space of the mosque prayer hall and to the words spoken by the humble and open-hearted man I had just met.

On the train home I started to read my new book, which detailed how and why Muslims do what they are meant to do – and also how and why in practice they do not always do it.[3] I never told my family or friends where I had been before the dinner: I felt I had briefly entered into a different space that might mean nothing to those around me.

Just before the end of my work placement Julian sent me yet another letter. He was enjoying his stay with relatives in Egypt while studying both colloquial and classical Arabic. For the first time in his life he had visited a mosque. And then he told me some other news: he had met someone else. She was a practising Muslim and Julian thought I might want to know that she was very petite. I didn't. I stopped reading about Islam and I stopped writing to him altogether.

Working on 'the Holy Land'

Two months later, I went to work with nine other English teenagers on a kibbutz in northern Galilee in Israel. The kibbutz was officially Jewish but did not take it too seriously: when the Orthodox Rabbi came to do a spot check, those of us working in kitchens scurried around to make sure the meat had been stored separately from the milk. I took part in the Jewish occasions although – like the other volunteers – without much sense of their meaning. For the celebratory festival of Purim, the kibbutz held a fancy-dress party: I went as Mickey Mouse.

We worked six days a week and could take three days consecutive leave a month. In my days off, I cycled around the Sea of Galilee, visiting the Church of the Loaves and Fishes, where the 'Feeding of the 5,000' could have taken place and the hill where Jesus is said to have delivered the Sermon on the Mount. I also tried to look inside the church in Capernaum, where Jesus preached and performed miracles but I wasn't allowed in: I wasn't modestly dressed enough.

I took the opportunity to travel further afield. The kibbutz organizers explained that it was safe to hitchhike as long as we never accepted a lift from a car with blue number plates, as those number plates signified the car belonged to Israeli citizens who were Arabs. We were young and consequently ignored their advice, gratefully accepting lifts from everyone.

Tempting discoveries

After hitchhiking to Tel Aviv, another volunteer and I caught an Arab bus to visit Jericho. The Arab buses were so much cheaper than the Israeli ones, although the shattered glass in the bus windows was a bit off-putting. The bus had to stop to let on armed Israeli soldiers who checked that everybody was travelling with the right permits; two men were thrown off the bus. When we arrived, we walked along the roads at the bottom of the Mount of Temptation. Some local Muslims spotted us – I could tell the woman was Muslim by her long clothes and headscarf – and invited us into their home for dinner. We accepted: we felt poor and hungry. But when they showed us around their home we realized there were only two chickens in their yard – and then they killed one of them for us. We received a delicious meal and gave nothing in return; they were left with one chicken. I went away feeling more than a little guilty.

The two of us headed by bus further south, to the caves of Qumran, famous for the 'Dead Sea Scrolls'.[4] In 1947, a group of children had stumbled upon the first set of tens of thousands of scroll fragments written in different languages. These scrolls had been dated to be a thousand years older than any previously known Hebrew texts of the Bible. In one of the scrolls, the title 'Son of God' had been used in relation to someone who wasn't Jesus. I had heard that the scrolls maintained an aura of intrigue: scholars agreed the finding was significant yet did not agree who produced the scrolls. But we soon discovered the caves themselves were now empty: there was nothing to see. We waited for hours until the next bus came along, standing with our backpacks on the side of the road, in the middle of this barren landscape of rocks and caves.

A wonderful religion?

After four months travelling around and working on the kibbutz I went backpacking to Egypt. I knew Julian would have moved on by then to Italy, to study Italian while staying with other relatives. In Egypt, like so many young British girls, I was harassed by the 'Muslim' men. I had fair hair and very few clothes: my trousers needed washing so I travelled around wearing shorts. I still had little understanding of Islamic culture and had no idea that it would have been marginally more respectful for me to wear my dirty trousers than my clean shorts and that it would have helped immensely if I had worn something over my hair.

I sat by the Nile, watching the world go by. An Egyptian man approached and, after establishing I was from England, volunteered his views on life in general and Islam in particular. 'Islam is a wonderful religion – we can marry four wives. And in Islam, we can divorce too, although God doesn't like it very much. So my plan is to go to England, marry four women, divorce them, and then marry another four.' It sounded bizarre. 'I don't suppose,' he added, hopefully, 'that you have a sister?'

University of life

At the end of my 'gap year', I wanted to skip university. I wanted to live simply like those I had come across in Israel and Egypt; I also wanted to do charity work, to do my little bit towards helping the world's poor and needy. I had a place to study economics at Cambridge: my father successfully persuaded me that it would not be a very sensible idea to throw this prospect away. And so I went to university.

University was a free-thinking, open-minded space where students had time to develop their own perspectives on politics, religion and everything else. At the Fresher's Fair for new students, I signed up to the student societies for all three major political parties. I also decided to join the Christian and Islamic societies.

I had always had an inner faith in God – but I wanted to question and understand this faith and the faith of those I had encountered. Why was my religion called 'Church of England' and not just Christianity anyway? Was my belief meant to have any impact on how I lived my life? Who were those people that I had met who called themselves Muslims? And did Islam really promote harassing women and having lots of wives?[5]

I became a member of the University Christian Association. I then looked for the University Muslim Association but that was not so simple. A Muslim student urged me not to join the Islamic Student Society; I must make sure I join the Student Islamic Society. When I eventually found the Muslim societies, I couldn't remember which one I was meant to join and which one I wasn't. It reminded me of the Monty Python film *Life of Brian*[6] – Brian is keen to join the Judean People's Front but people around him tell him that he really should be joining the People's Front of Judea.

Undeterred, I went along to an Islamic Society 'Squash', or reception, held to welcome new members. It was an isolating experience: everyone else was Muslim; I wasn't and had no intention of being one. I was just going there to see what it was like. The event was almost all male: a couple of people did make an attempt to make me feel welcome but seemed to be finding the situation awkward. I didn't immediately click with anyone: I thought that books might be a more useful way of finding out about Islam.

Bookworm

I found books pitting Islam against 'the West' as if there was no shared ground, usually extolling the virtues of Islam while blaming 'the West' – primarily women and their 'nakedness' – for all the world's evils. One 'put-down' of the West written by a Muslim was interesting: 'Western civilization has no clear identity, because it is a salad or cocktail civilization.'[7] The implication was that Muslims are better since they all apparently have the same monolithic identity – therefore there is no salad in 'their' civilization and certainly no cocktail.

I also discovered strident books about Islam and Muslims written by non-Muslims. One of these was given to me when I went with my friends from the Christian Society to a Christian-Muslim debate; most of the book discussed different reasons for why Muslims were so resistant to converting to Christianity. It concluded: 'It has seemed to those who have sought to save Muslims that Satan has made a special effort to hold them in his power.'[8] Yet I had understood that Muslims believed in God and had to do good deeds. It didn't seem very Satanic to me – I was obviously missing something.

I then read more straightforward accounts of the Muslim belief that explained how it affected Muslims both spiritually and practically in their daily life. The Muslim students around me had grown up with a children's book called *Islam: Beliefs and Teachings,*[9] which summarized it all in a short easy-to-read volume – one girl lent me her copy, which I found particularly useful at a time when I was surrounded by stacks of academic economics textbooks and journal articles.

In a nutshell

I found the core beliefs easy enough to understand.

Muslims believe in one God, Allah, the Creator and the Sustainer of the Universe, the All-knowing, the All-powerful, the Most Merciful. He makes the universe work in harmony, can give life and take it away, has always existed and will always exist. He has no needs: He does not eat and does not sleep. He has no partner or son. There is no other God.

Muslims believe in predestination: man's moral free will enables him to choose whatever course of action he wants but God knows all that will happen even before it happens.

Muslims believe that God sent 124,000 Prophets throughout time to diverse communities. Prophets taught the same essential message to all humanity: worship God and perform good deeds. Twenty-five prophets were mentioned by name in the Qur'an, starting with Adam, including Noah, Abraham, Moses and Jesus, and culminating with Muhammad, whom Muslims believe was sent to all mankind.

Muslims believe in all the revealed Books, including the Psalms of David, the Torah of Moses, the Gospel of Jesus and finally the Qur'an revealed to Muhammad.

Muslims believe in unseen Angels, including Angel Gabriel.

And Muslims believe in the Afterlife, believing that God would judge all humanity with mercy on the Day of Judgement, judging us on our belief in God and on our actions.

I was happy enough to understand these beliefs; I had no intention of ever adopting them as my own.

There were also five ritual acts of worship, the 'pillars' of faith, which formed an integral and unchangeable part of being Muslim. These pillars were called *shahadah*, *salah*, Ramadan, *zakat* and *Hajj*. They sounded very foreign.

The Muslim acts of worship started to make a little more sense once I understood their meaning in English: saying the creed, repeating it during prayer many times a day; praying five times a day; fasting from food and drink in daylight hours for one month a year; donating a proportion of their savings to charity once a year and making a pilgrimage to Mecca once in their lifetime. Muslims could do more of any of them but were not meant to do less. The rituals seemed designed to help Muslims remember their Creator frequently throughout the day, throughout the year and throughout their lives.

Living Islam

I read about how Muslims must live their faith through a wide range of daily actions. The focus was not only on their personal relationship with God but also on looking after their material and physical needs, including getting enough sleep. While Muhammad slept little at night, he encouraged a quick afternoon nap: I already did that in between lectures and occasionally during them.

And Muslims were meant to look outward:[10] showing lovingness towards children, being considerate to neighbours, reducing their wastefulness, helping to improve the community around them and striving towards social justice. My mother abseiled off a multi-storey car park to raise money for cancer research; my father used to make me go back to my room if I ever walked out of it forgetting to turn off the lights. My mother took me to visit old ladies with learning difficulties; my father headed a local community association. I had plenty of examples of Islamic actions within my own family.

The Islamic guidelines seemed comprehensive, logical and reasonable. Praying could be quick but had to be frequent. In Ramadan, Muslims had to fast until sunset but then had to rush to break their fast. Muslims had to offer the best hospitality to any visitor who dropped by for a day and a night and then look after them for a further two days; anything more was considered to be charity.[11] And if someone hit them, they could hit them back instead of turning the other cheek, but it would be infinitely better for them to forgive (42:40).

I discovered that Cambridge had a well-stocked Muslim book-shop, which included a whole section on women. I read how Islam actively encouraged education for boys and girls equally and there was no problem with women working.[12] I picked up titles like: *Womanpower: The Arab Debate on Women at Work* and *Beyond the Veil: Male-Female dynamics in Muslim Society.*[13] Fatima Mernissi, the author of the latter book, discussed Islam's positive attitude towards sexuality and concluded that women should be aiming much higher than simple equality than men. This woman certainly seemed to be going against the stereotypes.

Hating the Husseins

While I was immersed in my own little student life at university, the rest of the world was carrying on. Every morning I woke up to the *Today* programme on Radio 4. For years, during the morning drive to school, I had heard only the section that explained my girls' schedule for the day – my father always dropped me off at school before I got to hear any of the content. Now I could finally listen to the news.

It was 1991. Saddam Hussein had just invaded Kuwait, having already committed various atrocities against the Iranians and his own people in Iraq. Fortunately he was swiftly stopped by an American-led coalition. Thousands of these aggressive Iraqis were killed. Sadly, over 2,000 Iraqi civilians were also killed. That must have been the inevitable 'collateral damage'. I didn't hear much about any of their personal lives.

I found my shy Muslim friend, Asma Hussein, very upset near the pigeon holes where students picked up messages and flyers. She had started receiving hate mail from fellow students. Her surname was shared with Saddam; she was no relation.

Practise first

I found a few more Muslim girls to be friends with, although I didn't see much of them as they were either medics or lawyers. Still, when we did meet up, I felt very comfortable in their company.

I also decided to observe two of the Islamic practices.

Staying away from pork was easy to manage within a student diet that mainly consisted of pasta and omelettes and I thought it might even be good for me.

Giving up drinking was rather more challenging. Within Islam, there are clear guidelines on alcohol: Muslims are not allowed to drink it – not even one glass. The Qur'an says: 'Say: They will ask thee about intoxicants and games of chance. Say: "In both there is great evil as well as some benefit for man; but the evil which they cause is greater than the benefit which they bring"' (2:219). One of my economics friends ran the student bar: there was definitely profit in it, despite the drinks being so cheap.

I could see all around the effects that drinking was having: as an alcohol-filled evening progressed, people became more relaxed about flirting both with people that they knew and with people they had only just met. In the morning, the girls would discuss what they could remember of the night before; relationships were being made and broken overnight. I carried on going to the student parties anyway, even once bringing along a bottle of vodka to qualify for entry, but I was determined to prove to myself I could have a good time without drinking.

Apart from these minor lifestyle and social changes, I was not expecting Islam to affect my life. And then I went to join my family on holiday, where my father observed me drinking Coca-Cola while tucking into the pork chops.

I realized I should be able to explain my actions, both to others and myself. But I struggled. While I found the holistic logic of Islam compelling, at its core it just seemed so foreign. Muslims kept insisting on talking about Allah. I also knew next to nothing about this person called Muhammad.

Allah and the Last Prophet

To me, Allah sounded like a name given to a pagan idol. I could never see myself calling God Allah.

I discussed my thoughts with Patricia, a close student friend studying anthropology. I discovered that God is known by many names, both through time and across cultures. Netjer is the one God of Ancient Egypt. The Sudanese Dinka have one God known as Nhialic. I knew that other words for God included Deus in Latin, Dios in Spanish, and Gott in German but was taken aback to learn that Jews and Christians in Arabic-speaking countries called God Allah. The Hebrew Prophets called God Elohim; John the Baptist and Jesus used the Aramaic and Syriac Alaha. Elohim, Alaha and Allah even had the same meaning: 'the One who is worshipped'. There seemed to be an overwhelming belief across time and space in a single Supreme Power, despite this one God being described through numerous manifestations, attributes and names. After all, as Shakespeare said: 'What's in a name? That which is called a rose / By any other name would smell as sweet' (*Romeo and Juliet*: II, 2, 890–1).

Even once I had accepted there could be more than one word for

God, I was cautious to accept that Muhammad might have been given God's message. I had been brought up as a Christian; Muhammad was never even mentioned. I had ended up with the idea that Jesus was the last genuine religious leader – anyone else must be an impostor. But Muhammad was a real historical figure, of humble and illiterate origins who taught the people about a way of worship that was similar to but also different from the previously revealed monotheistic faiths in noticeable ways. He has had and continues to have a real impact on the daily practical and spiritual lives of millions and now over a billion people. How could I not know who he was?

I began to find out about Muhammad's life and his character and in the process learned more about many of the Prophets I knew from the Bible. I began to believe that he could be a Prophet after all.

A reluctant decision

Then in November 1991, during the first term of my second year at university, I was unable to sleep. I lay awake with thoughts circulating endlessly in my head.

I believed in God, an all-knowing and all-powerful God. But that meant if God was so all-powerful, He must be everywhere – and that meant God was with me, right then. So God could see me and God could see my innermost thoughts. That was really bad news. I had been trying to forget about those thoughts. I tossed and turned.

God would know I believed in Him and in all the Prophets. Yet I didn't see myself as religious – I wanted to believe in God and carry on with my life normally. I now saw that God would know that. And God would know that I never prayed to Him, I never thanked Him, I never even acknowledged Him. What kind of belief was that? My belief should be backed up by actions. But I didn't want to change – my life was comfortable. God would know that too.

I wanted to sleep and make the problem go away – but I couldn't. The hours passed by; the new day dawned. I was exhausted. I finally accepted that if I wanted to be true to my convictions, I would have to let my belief in God affect my life – if I didn't, I was only deceiving myself.[14] Very reluctantly, I submitted to God, in will, in heart and in mind. I remembered the Arabic word for 'a person who submits' is a *muslim*: I was becoming one of those.

I was also choosing not only to submit to God but to follow the teachings and example of Muhammad. I was choosing to become a Muslim with a capital 'M'. But I already believed in God and I already believed that Muhammad was the culmination of all Prophets sent before him. I didn't believe I had much of a choice any more.

A gentle start

Although I knew in my heart I was now a Muslim, I was not in a hurry to make it public. I wanted to start slowly.

I didn't know how to pray like other Muslims, but I believed God was merciful and I hoped He would know that I was doing my best. The next day, I sat on my bedroom carpet and read in English the seven verses of the first chapter of the Qur'an, *Surah Fatihah* – 'The Opening'. It seemed strikingly similar to the Lord's Prayer.

Praise be to God, the Most Kind, the Most Merciful,
Master of the Day of Judgement.
You alone do we worship,
You alone do we ask for help.
Show us the straight path, the path of those whom You have favoured,
Not the path of those who earn Your anger, nor of those who go astray. (1:1-7)

I now tried to fit five daily prayers into my life. Each prayer was short but it was a struggle to pray the full five in the designated time slots. In the next seven days, some days I managed two, some days three. One day, I found time to do four; I wondered if I could ever achieve five. A non-Muslim student friend discussed my situation with me: 'I don't know why you are stressing about it anyway,' she commented,

'I can think of so many better things to do with my time.' Yet in Islam, prayer was the most important pillar of the Muslim faith after the creed.

After a week of trying, I prayed five prayers, all at the 'proper' times. That very evening, the student Pakistani Society was holding their annual dinner at my college. It was pure coincidence – or was it purely God's will? I had joined the Society to meet more Muslims, and my student Muslim friends were all there. During the course of the meal, I mentioned my recent personal accomplishment to Sara, a medic. After the speeches, Sara and her friend Farhana told me that they both thought that evening should be the night for my 'conversion'. 'There's no time like the present,' said Farhana, a lawyer: 'What exactly are you waiting for?' I couldn't come up with a reason that would convince her I should delay.

Going public

Sara told me it was easy. I just needed to take a full shower, which included washing my hair, and then put on clean clothes. In the meantime she would gather some people together in my room. I could then say in front of them the Muslim creed, or *shahadah*: 'I bear witness that there is no God but God, and Muhammad is the Messenger of God.'

I went into the student shower block, knowing that this was the most symbolic shower I would probably ever have. Yet normal life was carrying on: a male student was in the all-female shower cubicles. Once he had left, I scrubbed and washed and started getting nervous. I came back to my college room, where my gentle friend Sabiha – another medic – was waiting. For a few minutes, we sat on the prayer mat she had brought with her and I practised the *shahadah*. The room filled up with other Muslims. Sabiha said the creed in Arabic and I repeated the words slowly, going bright red in the process. Everyone else was silent; no one commented on my pronunciation. It was all over in a few minutes. I was overwhelmed with embraces from the other female students; the men congratulated me warmly with words.

In my heart, I had said the *shahadah* the week before, when I was alone before God. But now it was public. Now it seemed a lot more real. There was no turning back.

The Hindu perspective

I went to talk over what had happened with my fellow economics student, Sriya, an Indian Hindu of the Brahmin caste. Sriya seemed to be able to empathize with what was happening in my life far more easily than the other English students could. She was happy to discuss both her faith and mine for hours.

I had come across Hinduism before – I thought I had learned the essentials from my religious education teacher at school. She had told us that Hindus worship a being with lots of arms and legs; and they often don't have running water so wash themselves using a cup and a bucket.

Sriya explained how, like Muslims, Hindus believe in one omnipotent and omnipresent God. But many Hindus found it easier to pray to God through a physical object – or two. Like Islam, Hinduism was a universal faith, believing that a set of divine rules have been sent for everyone to follow and live by, with these laws existing even before the creation of the universe. And like Islam, Hinduism didn't distinguish between 'secular' and 'religious' acts: every act was an act of worship if done with the right intention. Her Hindu daily prayers included the words: 'Like the rain water from the sky falls and flows to the same ocean, let all my prayers in every direction reach the same Almighty.' Amen to that.

I needed to cover my hair when I prayed – Sriya offered to come with me to buy my first scarf. We both learned that the Top Shop ones look beautiful but fall off if you are not going to pin them to your head.

Time to pray

To learn the full Muslim ritual prayer, or *salah*, I cycled to Sabiha's room in the centre of town for weekly lessons.[15] Twice along the way, I came across a lady walking by completely covered in black – she looked very scary and I sped up.

Sabiha explained that each prayer was divided into sets of prescribed movements called *raka'ah*. Each *raka'ah* involved standing, reciting *Surah Fatihah* and sometimes another chapter in Arabic, bowing down and prostrating in a position known as *sujud*. I carefully wrote down everything I needed to do, along with the English translation of each Arabic word.

As I moved between the different positions, I just had to say two words: *Allahu Akbar*: 'God is Great'. *Sujud* was a challenge as I attempted to read my crib-sheet while my nose and forehead were on the floor. Yet that same *sujud* position was also the most natural: I had never before experienced feeling complete humbleness before God.

At the end of the prayer, I had to turn to the left and right saying: 'Peace be upon you, and God's blessings' to those all around me, near or far. I knew when I reached this part that I had managed to get all the way through to the end. Or it might merely mean that I had been reading the wrong part of my notes.

When I had finally learned the whole prayer, a Christian friend told me that she felt it was ritualistic and meaningless. I agreed that it was ritualistic but to me it had as much meaning as I wanted to give it.

Each to their own

My non-Muslim student friends were generally ambivalent about my decision to become Muslim: it didn't affect them and as far as they could see I hadn't changed, either on the inside or the outside. My clothing hadn't altered: it was winter, so everyone was well wrapped up. As I only wore the Muslim headscarf when I was praying, no one knew I was Muslim unless I chose to tell them.

The committee of Student Community Action, an umbrella volunteering organization, started to become positively enthusiastic about me being Muslim once I won a bottle of champagne through their prize draw and asked them to keep it. However, the group of evangelical Christian friends with whom I had become friendly were very disappointed in my decision: they felt I had defected. When I helped at a student-run camp for underprivileged children, I came across a training manual lying on the bunk bed of my fellow helper and friend Elaine. It was full of tips about how to convince Muslims about Christianity so that Muslims too could reach Paradise. None of my Muslim friends owned an equivalent manual. Perhaps Muslims didn't try so hard to 'save' everyone: after all, Muslims weren't sure if they would be going off to Paradise themselves. Or perhaps Muslims were just less organized.

Facing the family

In my first university holidays as a Muslim I went back to my parent's home.

Julie, who was back in the UK at another university, was being supportive and mildly positive about my decision to be Muslim, particularly as it helped her with the family dynamics: she had now become the well-behaved daughter and I had become the rebel. And I was able to supply her with a few choice quotes from the Qur'an for her dissertation on the subject of the immigration of Turkish Muslims to the Netherlands. Later, when we both moved to London, she found out about the obligation of Muslims to be hospitable and appeared with armfuls of washing.

William was still young: my parents now asked me never to discuss Islam with him. I didn't. But whenever my little brother saw me praying with a headscarf on, he mimicked the actions while wearing a tea-towel over his head. He thought this was a great game – especially when he could see how desperate I was to grab the cloth off him before another family member could see. I continued to pray all the ritual prayers, although I stopped mid-prayer if I heard my parents coming up the stairs.

Unsurprisingly, my parents were the most affected by my decision.

Changing my mind

My mother was initially worried that I had been brainwashed. She asked me if I was going to give away the few possessions I owned to this new group I had come across. My father knew a bit about Islam in the UK – and knew that most Muslims weren't white and that the British Muslim community was generally a poor one. He was right. But those two facts were unrelated to each other and were also unrelated to being Muslim – there are plenty of wealthy Muslims of all colours to be found in the UK and worldwide. Unfortunately, the poor English language skills of the local Indian shopkeeper simply furthered the idea that Islam was a 'foreign' faith – although of course the shopkeeper might have been Hindu; they weren't sure.

My mother also asked me how was it possible to be Muslim when I had been confirmed into the Church of England just six years before. But I was only 14 then. I had dressed completely in white, enjoyed a delicious lunch at home with my family and godparents afterwards, and had been given some wonderful and long-lasting presents, including the *Shorter Oxford English Dictionary*. Beforehand, I had sat through a sequence of lessons led by the local village vicar to make sure my peers and I were suitably prepared. The vicar made sure we had understood the concept of the Trinity: he pretended to be drunk, staggering behind the sofa, to demonstrate how one person can take different forms in different circumstances. I subsequently spent many school break-times pacing around my classroom, trying to remember the Christian creed word for word in preparation for the ceremony. At that tender age, it would have been very unusual to have challenged the vicar even if I had wanted to – which I didn't. I had been convinced.

And now I had changed my mind. My father thought it was just a phase.

Family values

My mother was devastated. I felt bad: Muslims were told specifically not to upset their parents – particularly their mother. It said in the Qur'an: 'Now (among the best of the deeds which) We have enjoined upon man is goodness towards his parents. In pain did his mother bear him, and in pain did she give him birth' (46:15). In another verse about parents, it said: '… always speak unto them with reverent speech, and spread over them humbly the wings of thy tenderness, and say: "O my Sustainer! Bestow thy Grace upon them, even as they cherished and reared me when I was a child"' (17:23–24).

For years, my mother had cared for me, as a baby, as a child and as a maturing adult. Now she thought I was rejecting the way she had brought me up. She thought she was losing me. She thought she had failed.

While I was keeping the values that my parents had brought me up with – like honesty, the importance of marriage, and the emphasis on helping others – the few practical changes I was choosing to make seemed to be more of an issue than any theological differences. No more wine – not even a sip to make a toast to someone on a special occasion? And no more pork – not even those tasty little chipolatas wrapped in bacon that came out at Christmas time? My father managed a company that sold pork scratchings, mainly to pubs – I was not going to be his biggest consumer.

Has somebody died?

I came across several letters of condolence lying around the study, addressed to my parents. 'How terrible for you', wrote one lady whom I knew well: she used to babysit me when I was a child. I thought somebody might have died – until I continued reading. Nobody had died. She was writing about me.

I felt incredibly alone. None of my Muslim friends were around to talk to and there were no other Muslims in my family. I needed to talk to God. It said in the Qur'an: 'Call unto your Sustainer humbly, and in the secrecy of your hearts' (7:55). In Islam, this was called 'making *dua*', supplicating to God.[16] I knew I could supplicate to God on my own or with others, any time, anywhere, in any language. I just had to make sure that I kept the palms of my hands facing upwards, 'open to receive God's blessings' as one Muslim girl had explained it to me, and say 'Amen' at the end, affirming the truth of what I had just said.

At home, in the quiet of the night, I spoke to God in English. I asked God to make this time of my life easier for me and I asked God for patience. And I found solace in another verse of the Qur'an: 'God does not burden any human being with more than he is well able to bear' (2:286).

My parents accepted my decision to be Muslim, albeit with mixed emotions. None of us knew that was really just the beginning.

2   Marriage Ties and Scarves

'And among His wonders is this: He creates for you mates out of your own kind so that you might incline towards them, and He engenders love and tenderness between you: in this, behold, there are messages indeed for people who think!'

(Qur'an 30:21)

'When a man gazes at his wife and she gazes at him, God looks at them both with a gaze that is compassion and mercy.'

(Saying of Muhammad)

I noticed that Muslim students behaved in a reserved manner around the opposite sex. Physical contact was non-existent, social conversation was limited and a male student never dropped by to chat one-to-one in a female student's room. I had various male non-Muslim university friends, and they came to my room to chat at any time of day or evening; it didn't seem like a big deal. And then my friend Matt came to visit.

Matt arrived drunk, threw up in the toilet next to my room and proceeded to crash out on my bed. He smelt terrible and was too heavy to move; I slept on the floor. He left in the early hours of the morning and brought me some chocolates to apologize later that day. I started to be more careful about whom I let in.

Kevin the Muslim

I had not been Muslim for long, and I wanted to be able to talk about it with someone of either sex who would understand. I was introduced to Khalid, an English man who had accepted Islam several years earlier and who was now head of the University Islamic Society. Khalid was happy to have a conversation but thought it would be easier for us both if other Muslim students did not see us get together. I wondered what those same Muslim students would have thought if they had seen Matt emerge from my room a few nights earlier. After Khalid had led the Friday congregational prayer in a student hall, I followed him at a discreet distance to his room and arrived in his room several minutes after him, as planned. Khalid kept the door open throughout the conversation.

I knew why Muslim men and women hesitated to talk together in private. There was a *hadith*, a saying of Muhammad, that whenever a man and a woman who were not closely related were alone in a room, there was always a third person present – Satan or temptation.[1] I could see there was wisdom in that. If I stopped having private chats with my male friends and if those friends also followed the Islamic limits on alcohol then presumably I wouldn't be ending up with drunk men on my bed.

Khalid explained what had led him to Islam, how his family had reacted and what life had been like for him since. He also clarified why he had changed his name. Khalid used to be called Kevin and, while the name had a good meaning – meaning both 'handsome' and 'beloved' in the original Gaelic – he couldn't imagine being a Muslim named Kevin.

It was a relief to meet someone else who had decided to make such an adjustment and who still seemed normal with a sense of humour. I left in good spirits, and went back to my room alone.

My first Muslim again

Julian's plans with the petite Muslim Egyptian hadn't worked out: after Italy, he had moved on to stay with family friends in France and she had stayed where she was. Julian and I were at separate universities; we saw each other just twice in our first year of college. Julian seemed different after his time in Egypt: he came across as much more serious and politically aware.

When I went to my family home for the start of the first year summer holidays I spoke to my mother about how Julian had changed. I told her frankly: 'I don't think I like him any more.' And then Julian telephoned.

Julian was looking for a fourth person to make up a group to travel around Europe. I had not made any other holiday plans and my mother and I agreed that if I was part of a mixed group I would be able to travel more safely. Julian's brother Jeffery was going with us too. I think Jeffery also knew the *hadith* about two people not being alone together: he spent a good portion of the holiday making sure that he accompanied us everywhere we went. He even stood between us on the deck of the ferry on the way back.

Despite Jeffery's best efforts to keep us apart, Julian and I discovered that not only our values but our beliefs were becoming increasingly compatible. And I was starting to like him again. In fact, I liked him a lot. As we got off the train in Spain, Julian said to me: 'I think we should probably get married.' I think that was a proposal.

A marriageable age?

Back at university, now in my second year, I waited my turn at one of the college telephone booths. In the early evening, I spoke to my mother and explained – with no preamble – that I would like to get married, preferably sooner rather than later. I didn't anticipate her response.

'Are you pregnant?' my mother asked. I assured her I wasn't. My mother was relieved she would have a little more time to think about our conversation. 'I really can't talk about this now,' she told me. 'William has just mentioned he is expected to bring a boxful of food for the Harvest Festival first thing tomorrow morning and I've also got a pile of ironing to do.' I 'phoned back after two hours, hoping she may have finished all her jobs. 'But I didn't think you even liked Julian,' she remembered. 'Anyway, Daddy isn't here right now; I will have to discuss this with him later.'

Two days later, I received a letter from my father. He told me that a marriage works best if both the husband and wife live in the same place. He explained that with marriage came responsibilities: the husband should bear the economic responsibility for his wife. And he asked if my prospective husband was planning to pay the rest of my university fees. It wasn't what I wanted to hear: I threw the letter away.

We all took a little time to calm down. My mother continued to object to my youth. 'You know, Lucy,' she said, 'Even if you marry immediately after you graduate, you will only be twenty-one.'

I pointed out to my mother that she was only twenty-one when she got married; she told me times had changed. They had. Now women were not marrying until an average age of twenty-nine.[2] When I was at secondary school, it was a big social taboo to have been born outside marriage – we had all known who the few 'illegitimate children' were. And now nearly half of all children in the UK were being born to couples who weren't married.[3] Times had indeed changed – but Islam hadn't.

Within Islam, it was clear that the only legitimate sexual relationship, and legitimate way to have and to bring up children, was within marriage between a man and a woman. This meant that having a boyfriend, girlfriend or partner who was anything more than 'just a friend' did not qualify as Islamic behaviour. The Qur'an said: 'They (wives) are as a garment for you and you (husbands) are as a garment for them' (2:187). Muhammad said: 'Marriage is half the faith.' Julian and I wanted to be married.

Eventually it was agreed we would have our wedding as soon as we had graduated.

The bedroom ceremony

The first thing Julian and I did was to celebrate.

In Cambridge, I was in a tutorial discussion about the economics of the housing market with a professor and just one other student. It was Friday afternoon and I asked to leave early: I said I wasn't feeling very well. I cycled to the bus station with only minutes to spare before the bus left to Julian's university town. Three hours later, Julian met me as agreed and we walked to his student room to find two of his male friends waiting, together with his brother.

Julian had arranged a short ceremony in his student bedroom, called a *nikah*, which as Muslims we believed would be valid in the eyes of God. Neither of us had ever seen a *nikah* before. His parents weren't around although they knew about it: they were thousands of kilometres away, having moved on from Kenya to live in Saudi Arabia.

The *imam*, the religious leader, arrived at Julian's room. He had an Arabic name. He found it hard to remember my name as it was unfamiliar to him; for the same reason I found it hard to remember his. He reminded us of the importance of marriage in Islam and of the need to show both love and mercy towards each other. The *imam* asked us each separately if we wanted to be married and he checked that we both had a representative or guardian, known in Arabic as a *wali*.[4] Julian was allowed to be his own representative; I could represent myself only if I had been through a divorce, so instead Julian selected his brother for the job. Jeffery and I laughed about his role as my wally.

The *imam* then wanted to know what Julian was giving me as a *mahr*, or dowry[5] – an unconditional present that we had to agree upon and which could be of any value, great or small. Julian was prepared: he had bought me a well researched, readable translation of the Qur'an[6] written by an Austrian convert and scholar called

Muhammad Asad. The original Arabic, the very same words that Muslims believe were revealed by Angel Gabriel in the seventh century to Muhammad, appeared alongside the English. Julian had absent-mindedly left the price sticker on: it had cost him the enormous sum of £26.

The bird and groom

The *imam* was satisfied that all of the contractual conditions of the *nikah* had been fulfilled. He presented us each a Muslim marriage certificate, which we signed along with the two witnesses. When I read it through, I was horrified to see a rather unfortunate typing error: the certificate was addressed to the 'the bird and groom'.

Julian's friends and brother hugged him; I knew they wouldn't be hugging me as all of them were male. I emerged from his room to be congratulated by the two strongly Christian English girls with whom Julian shared a student house; they had thoughtfully bought us a little cake. We all enjoyed a few mouthfuls before going out for dinner.

I could have invited my family; I could have arranged my own representative who was not related to Julian; and I could have invited my own friends along. A *nikah* was meant to be a fully open and public commitment to marriage; our quiet *nikah* was not ideal.

But I didn't do any of those things.

I had imagined that my parents would dismiss the ceremony as being neither necessary nor valid: a *nikah* wasn't recognized in English law. I had not been involved in organizing the *nikah*: I had said the Muslim creed, the *shahadah*, only weeks before and I was still working on how to pray. I also had a stream of essays due to be handed in – I did think it was fortunate I was not being officially examined in my subject that year as I was getting very little work done. And the Cambridge terms were so short that I felt I couldn't ask anyone from there – particularly a medic – to take a weekend out to join me for the occasion.

My God and yours

I came back to university a bit shell-shocked. The first person I bumped into at the college entrance hall was Rebecca, one of my evangelical Christian friends.

Rebecca told me she had just got engaged and held out her left hand to show me the ring. I knew her husband-to-be – he was studying theology and had spent an intense evening with Rebecca and me when I was investigating both Islam and Christianity. He had explained how words from the Bible were translated from the Latin, which was derived from the Greek, which was derived from Hebrew and Aramaic: it had all sounded mind-blowingly complicated. But I was happy for Rebecca.

I thought Rebecca might also be happy for me, so I told her that I had just got married in the eyes of God. She responded sharply: 'But you haven't got married in the eyes of my God.' I had thought my God and her God were the same.

While I returned to my neglected studies, I simultaneously listened to the radio. I was bemused about what was going on in Algeria. The largest opposition party known as the FIS, the Islamic Salvation Front, had just had won 188 seats in the Assembly, while the original political party, the FLN, only won 15. The FLN government then banned the FIS. It didn't seem very democratic. Yet it was the major news story: the European experts being interviewed on Radio 4 explained that the cancelling of the elections was the right thing to do in those particular political circumstances. And I had thought my own life was complicated.

Thinking of the postman

I mentioned to my mother that I was keeping my maiden name upon marriage. 'Whatever will the postman think?' she asked. I wasn't sure that the postman cared.

I had a bewildering array of choices.[7] Under British law, I could use my current surname; use my husband's surname; add on his surname to mine to create a triple-barrelled monster; or I could even invent a brand new 'meshed' surname. But I wanted to keep my own.

I knew that the overwhelming majority of women in the UK changed their surname to their husbands' name; in the USA, four out of five did.[8] It seemed sexist to me: why didn't the man consider changing his? Until just over 100 years ago in England, I found out that all of a woman's wealth before marriage – and even her earnings after marriage – belonged to her husband: a woman was legally a minor, the property of her husband and it was only logical to take his surname.[9] I wasn't Julian's property, either in current English law or within Islamic law and, even if surname changing was now more a sign of love and commitment, I wanted to keep the name with which I had been born.

Years later I was invited to an English wedding, which took name-changing discussions to an entirely new level. My full name was written on the individual place card marking where I was seated. But women who had changed their surnames upon marriage found they were now named not only with their husband's surname but with his first name too. The tables were full of coordinated couples with names like Mr John Smith and Mrs John Smith. At least it meant I didn't have to remember so many names – but funnily enough the woman near me didn't like being called John. I saw the same thing in the *Tatler* magazine in the dentist's waiting room: the women in the photographs were captioned with their title followed by their husband's full name. It must be very high-class in England to lose not just one but both names.

Wedding bells

The wedding party preparations began. Julian and I had never ever been to a wedding; my mother hadn't attended one for years. But, undaunted, my mother appeared in Cambridge with her wedding briefcase, and booked the hall, the accommodation, the food, the flowers, the photography and the car. Julian and I left her to it – we had our final exams looming – but we still had a few opinions.

Julian had a strong view about children: he was adamant that children should attend. That was an issue: English weddings don't usually include children. I had never thought about it before. On reflection, I found that English custom slightly odd – given that one of the traditional functions of weddings was to enable a couple to have 'legitimate' children. And so we agreed we would invite children – my mother arranged for them all to eat jelly and ice cream.

Alcohol was an issue. Julian and I believed God clearly forbade us not only to drink alcohol but even to have anything to do with it.[10] Surely it would be reasonable to follow these guidelines at our own wedding? I thought my parents might be delighted that we were proposing significant savings on the wedding budget but their main concern was to ensure that everybody would be able to enjoy themselves fully. We discussed it and eventually agreed on an alcohol-free wedding. They said their friends wouldn't come if there wasn't alcohol. We said we wouldn't come if there was. It looked like it was going to be a very quiet wedding. My parents list upon a solution: my mother ordered in large quantities of elderflower champagne. We were then left with an unexpected problem: the wedding cake, which was traditionally made with alcohol. After much thought, the cake lady found a way to adapt her recipe. We were all relieved.

Revealing all

We also needed to sort out what everyone would wear on the day.

I had started to wear long-sleeved tops, teamed with full-length trousers or jeans. Muhammad said 'Every religion has a characteristic and the characteristic of Islam is modesty.'[11]

If I had been born 50 years earlier, I believed my new-found reluctance to wear shorts and T-shirts wouldn't have seemed so strange. Women in Victorian times played tennis in full-length dresses. At school, I learned about the individual Victorian bath-houses that were on wheels, so that people could be wheeled down to the sea and slip into the water in their long swimsuits without revealing anything. I also learnt about Gandhi who went to meet a fully-dressed King George V at Buckingham Palace in 1931 in his usual *dhoti* loincloth: he was described by Churchill as the 'half-naked Fakir' of India. One journalist asked him: 'Don't you feel embarrassed to see the King George V in this scanty dress?' Gandhi replied: 'Why should I feel ashamed? The King has enough on for both of us.'

But times had changed: wearing lots of clothes didn't always seem so normal any more. I only found a few verses mentioning dress in the Qur'an. One of the most specific verses was addressed to both men and women.

> Tell the believing men to lower their gaze and to be mindful of their chastity: this will be most conducive to their purity – (and,) verily, God is aware of all that they do. And tell the believing women to lower their gaze and to be mindful of their chastity, and not to display their charms (in public) beyond what may (decently) be apparent thereof; hence, let them draw their head-coverings over their bosoms. (24:30-31)

I concluded that modesty for men and women consisted of two things: being modest 'on the outside' in terms of clothing and – equally importantly – being modest 'on the inside' in terms of non-flirtatious behaviour.

It's in the detail

The detail about appropriate dress codes was tucked away within further *hadiths*. The obligations didn't fully apply until puberty, when young people were considered responsible for their actions.

I found out that Muslim men were meant to wear clothes that covered the area between the navel and the knee in front of all men and women except their spouse. I couldn't then understand why certain football teams from 'Muslim countries' allowed shorts that were shorter than that – but the authorities were probably too busy focusing on the female dress requirements to notice what the men wore. When women were with other women they also had to cover up fully only between the navel and the knee; around men who weren't close family they needed to cover up their arms, legs and body shape.[12]

It was only after I had taken some of my partially covering clothes to the local charity shop that I discovered Muslim women would happily wear casual short-sleeved tops – or 'dress up' in strapless low-cut dresses – when in front of other women or their husbands. It was an expensive discovery: it was too late to buy my clothes back.

I did find it all rather one-sided that so much of the Islamic dress-code obligations fell on women rather than men. But I also found it rather one-sided that both men's and women's magazines focused on what women looked like rather than men. Perhaps we were just naturally more beautiful. Julian bought me an interesting book called *Brainsex*[13] – it was about the biological differences between men and women both in the brain and elsewhere and the related emotional differences. I couldn't deny we were different: my mother hired Julian's wedding 'tails' over the telephone without him even turning up in the store; I definitely needed to go to the shops – and not just once.

Bridal wear

My 'going away' outfit was hard to find, especially given that it was British summer time. My mother and I were simply searching for a skirt that was full length and a top that was both long-sleeved and not see-through. It was a challenge. When I showed what we had found to a family friend, he commented that I looked like Margaret Thatcher. I was not sure that was a compliment.

And then my mother and I went shopping for a wedding dress. I found one quickly but it needed adjusting. Islamically, the length was fine: the flowing 'meringue' dress touched the floor with plenty of material to spare. But I didn't want the dress to have a low neckline; it was also sleeveless and I needed it to have 'arms'. The owner of the bridal wear shop was more than happy to arrange the changes, particularly as my mother was paying.

At the shop, I stepped out of the changing room wearing the wedding dress. I then tried on a traditional bridal veil. I thought the veil was pointless: it was made of transparent netting and didn't cover up anything. But when my mother saw me wearing the veil her eyes filled with tears. To her, I now looked like a 'real' English bride.

A little piece of cloth

I wanted to wear the Muslim headscarf permanently from the moment the wedding started. But it was asking a lot of my parents: my parents had accepted I was Muslim; they had accepted I wanted to marry a Muslim; they had even accepted I was adapting the way I dressed. Now I was asking them to accept the most public sign of all – the scarf – and in front of all their friends.

I had made the decision to cover my hair after reading various interpretations of the Qur'an and *hadith*. I had concluded it was an essential albeit small part of the modest dress Muslims should observe. It was – rather ironically – meant to help focus men's attention on what a woman said rather than what a woman looked like.

I was finding it hard to find the right time to change such a visible part of my appearance and to me the wedding seemed like it would be the perfect time: all our family and friends would be there, they could see I was not 'oppressed' and none of them would then be taken aback the next time they saw me. And I felt that if I couldn't do what I wanted to on the day that I became publicly married and fully 'grown up' then there would never be the right time to do it.

I felt I was definitely born in the wrong era. The Virgin Mary and all the other women of her time used to cover their hair without making a big issue of it, and no-one ever minded when five-year-old girls donned tea-towels to cover their hair during the Nativity Play. I had read that it was customary for Christian women to cover their hair in Europe and America until the nineteenth century; of course nuns still do. And so did some of my Granny's friends. But mainstream European traditions had changed from scarves to bonnets to hats[14] and then had changed again to wearing hats only in church or at special occasions. I was out of date.

Compromising times

In my parent's kitchen, I spoke with my mother and mother-in-law about my plans to wear the scarf. My mother told me she didn't want me to wear it at the wedding: she felt it would ruin the day. My mother-in-law told me she didn't want me to wear it either. 'Think about your mother, Lucy,' she urged me. 'This is your mother's special day – all of her friends are going to be there.' But this was going to be my special day too. I felt no one was supporting me. I cried in front of them and I left the room to cry alone.

My father came to speak to me and told me how upset my mother was getting. He also explained why. He told me: 'If you wear the scarf at the very start of the wedding, then this will be perceived by us – and by our friends – as rejecting all you previously stood for. But if you wear it when you say goodbye at the end, it will simply come across as part of an exciting and gentle transition into your new life.' I didn't understand how that one little piece of cloth could be laden with such great meaning. But we clearly needed to compromise.

I agreed I would wear the English transparent veil for most of the wedding to make my mother happy. And I would wear a scarf during the ceremony and from the end of the wedding party onwards to make me happy. My mother-in-law said she would be responsible for choosing a scarf, and for making sure that it matched the colour and material of my dress. The crisis was resolved.

Wedding jobs

I had very little to organize but I did have to find a wedding ring for Julian. I was pleased he wanted to wear one but I knew the ring would have to be silver:[15] according to Islam, both gold and silk were luxuries that women were allowed to wear but not men. Yet the local jeweller stocked only gold rings. 'How about this one?' he asked me, proffering a ring that looked silver but turned out to be white gold. Eventually, I ordered a simple but genuinely silver ring, which arrived just one week before the wedding.

My parents left the two of us to arrange the ceremony. We had already had our small *nikah* ceremony, which meant we were Islamically married and we were going to be having a small registry office reception to make us legally married. But we wanted to hold an additional ceremony so that we could affirm our marriage vows in front of all our family and friends – and so that we could have the wedding I had always imagined.

As a child, I had dreamed of a 'white' wedding, where I would be wearing a white dress and walking next to my father up the aisle of a church. So I approached the vicar of my college church to see if we could have the ceremony in the chapel. I mentioned that we would just need to take the statues of Jesus out of the church temporarily, as Muslims weren't allowed statues. It wasn't the best idea I had ever had. Why on earth would he adapt his Christian church to suit the requirements of a Muslim? He wouldn't: he politely declined the proposal.

The chaplain then said to me: 'I don't know much about Islam – can you tell me what it is all about?' I was caught by surprise partly because I had assumed that he knew the basics already and partly because I was now busy stressing about alternative venues. I quickly told him about the five ritual acts of worship. I completely neglected to mention the articles of faith – including the core and uniting belief in the one universal God. 'So it's just about actions, then,' he commented and held open the door for me to leave.

I found a new location for our wedding ceremony: my college gardens. I only had to make sure that no students were planning to hold wild parties in the garden that day.

And Julian found an experienced Muslim community leader named Basil to officiate. But three months before the wedding, Basil told Julian he was unable to be there. My father remained unfazed: 'Don't worry,' he said, obligingly. 'I can be the *imam*.' It was a sweet thought but we didn't take him up on his offer. Julian found another Muslim who was happy to preside over it. Together, the three of us agreed what he would say. But we forgot to discuss what he should wear.

A dream coming true?

The day before the main occasion, the two families gathered at the registry office where the marriage was officially made legal. I wore a hat for the event; it was all over in 20 minutes. I was glad I still had the wedding party to look forward to.

At the wedding, the new *imam* turned up in an Arab *thobe* – a long white tunic – topped with red and white headgear. We had only ever seen him bare headed and wearing jeans before. I was horrified: I had been expecting him to come in a suit and tie – I had wanted him to prove to the mainly non-Muslim guests how 'normal' *imams* could be. There was nothing we could do about it: under his *thobe,* he was wearing jeans. And when Julian asked him why he had chosen a *thobe*, the *imam* explained he had considered it very carefully. 'I thought this would be what the non-Muslim guests would expect,' he added. He was right: my mother told me he fitted her image of an *imam* perfectly.

The photographer wanted a picture of the bride accompanied by the *imam* on one side and the groom on the other. Yet the *imam* kept trying to stand as far away from me as possible. He didn't want to be any nearer: we weren't married. The photographer didn't understand and kept pushing us together. We ended up in a cosy little threesome, with the *imam* firmly holding the Qur'an between me and him.

When it was time for the ceremony, I felt my childhood dreams were finally coming true. I was wearing a traditional English ivory 'meringue-style' wedding dress, albeit accessorized with an ivory headscarf. While one of my parents' friends played Wagner's Bridal Chorus on the piano, I was walking up the aisle with my father by my side. Actually, I wasn't walking, I was running: my father is a big man who takes some very big strides. And the aisle was a path in a sunken garden surrounded by beautifully tended flower beds. My parents and I were learning to be flexible.

During the public ceremony the *imam* explained how we should be 'garments' for each other: a source of protection, of comfort and of warmth. He detailed some of our rights and duties.[16] Julian had the duty to support me and any children we went on to have. I retained my right to education and work and I simply had to support him emotionally. As the children ran around the gardens, the adult guests listened quietly and politely. No one mentioned the scarf.

Cultural exchange

I swapped my scarf for the bridal veil, and took my place in the reception line, taking turns to greet everyone at the wedding. We had guests from a variety of countries: the UK, France, Holland, Germany, Italy, America, Venezuela, Oman and Saudi Arabia. When each person approached, I just waited to see what would happen. Some kissed me twice, some three times, some four of which three had to be on the same cheek, some shook hands, and some made no physical contact. A few Muslim men stood opposite me awkwardly, clearly wishing they were somewhere else – they didn't want to make the standard comment about how beautiful the bride was looking; if I really was that beautiful they should be looking away.

A number of guests had not replied to the wedding invitation but came anyway. Many Muslims were used to holding large weddings, which did not adhere to a strict headcount and so did not necessitate a reply. The Americans – Muslim and non-Muslim – had noticed that a stamped addressed envelope hadn't been included and so thought a reply was not wanted. Two of the invited guests did not turn up, but sent others in their place; another couple brought extra people. And so the highly organized seating plan and individual place names at each table did not work out exactly as planned. But, although my mother found the uncertainty stressful, everybody did find a place to eat. And everybody seemed to be having a good time – despite the lack of alcohol.

The waitresses distributed the bottom two layers of the tiered wedding cake; I asked them to preserve the top layer. The English tradition was to serve this cake at the Christening of the first child. I wasn't planning to have a Christening but thought that one day the cake might come in useful.

At the end of the meal, we found a huge amount of elderflower champagne was left over. Many of those who weren't Muslim had stayed away from it as it wasn't alcoholic; many of those who were Muslim had stayed away from it in case it was.

Leaving family and friends

I left all the guests in order to go with my mother to change into my going-away outfit and scarf. She had arranged to have the student room next door to the college dining hall set aside for that purpose and had given Jeffery the keys to look after.

But we couldn't get into the room; it was locked. It was locked from the inside. I couldn't understand why. I started banging on the door. My mother was getting increasingly tense: there was a schedule to follow and Julian and I had a train to catch. Ten minutes later, Jeffery emerged, along with some of the student guests. They had turned the room into a prayer room. Julian and I should have thought about providing a prayer room for the Muslims but we hadn't – and Jeffery had improvised.

I quickly dressed in my 'going away' clothes and put on my scarf. I rushed to join Julian who was waiting next to the chauffeur-driven wedding car. Once again, no one mentioned the scarf: the guests wished us well, blew kisses and smiled. But Julian's 11-year-old brother Daniele broke down in tears and clung to Julian as he got into the car: Daniele thought that now his brother was married, he would be leaving his family forever.

But Julian wasn't leaving anyone – and nor was I. He was just adding another dimension to his life – and so was I.

The wedding car whisked the two of us away. Ten minutes later, we stepped out of the chauffeur-driven Bentley at the local train station – we were more used to arriving by bicycle. Julian and I headed straight for the ticket counter and bought tickets to London. We made sure we received the full discount for student travel.

3 On Foreign Soil

'O man! Behold, We have created you all out of a male and a female, and have made you into nations and tribes, so that you might come to know one another.'

(Qur'an 49:13)

'Be in this world as though you were a stranger or a traveller.'[1]

(Saying of Muhammad)

People warned me not to get married young: I should first see the world. I couldn't understand why I couldn't do both. After all, I now had a partner with whom to see it. Julian and I decided to explore the Middle East together during the second of our long university summer holidays, after our *nikah*. We took a cheap charter flight to Turkey and then planned one day at a time.

Visible differences

As we walked through the streets of Istanbul, I noticed the variety in women's dress. Some women wore scarves and long tops, some were dressed all in black and some were in mini-skirts. No one looked twice at each other's outfits. And why should they? Their choice of dress was personal. But at Istanbul University there were no scarves in sight. Wearing a scarf as a religious symbol at schools and university was outlawed in secular Turkey. I was glad that our British universities placed rather more importance on the intelligence of their students than their dress sense.

In Turkey, I started wearing a scarf too: I thought it would be a good place to experiment. I was wearing it as I popped into the local bakery to get some fresh bread rolls. The ageing baker was delighted to see me in my scarf. '*Alhamdulillah*,' he said in Arabic, gesturing to my head. I knew that meant 'Praise be to God' – I was pleased that I had made him so happy. But on the third day of our stay, I appeared without my scarf – I had just washed my hair and wanted it to dry. The baker waved his arms at me and shook his head; he looked so sad. I wanted to explain that I had only ever been practising – but I couldn't speak Turkish and he couldn't speak English. I bought our bread and left. I resolved to become more consistent – I didn't want to upset anyone else. And I soon discovered that my wet hair dried even under a scarf.

Julian and I left Istanbul that evening by bus, and arrived 12 hours later in Göreme, in central Turkey. We visited an ancient church, where some of the different frescoes on the walls were still visible. We found Jesus depicted in blue boxer shorts, flying like Superman to rescue Adam from Hell. Other images were not so vivid: some had been worn down by time or covered in mould but some had been scratched out years ago by Muslims in the area. In Muslim places of worship, it was clear: no pictures or statues of people – particularly Prophets – were permitted. The Muslim buildings were decorated with other art forms such as geometrical patterns and calligraphy. I knew this was to ensure people focused on worshipping the one God. But it didn't seem very tolerant to go around defacing the images in other people's places of worship. The Qur'an had taught us to say: 'Unto you your moral law, and unto me, mine' (109:6).

Land of peace

From Göreme, another bus took us to Antakya on the Turkish-Syrian border – and we were left to walk through 'no-man's land' to Syria.

My parents had warned us to be careful in Syria: they had heard from the BBC News that it was in a state of war. But the chief officer at passport control in Aleppo clearly wasn't aware of it. *Assalamu Alaikum.* 'Welcome to Syria, land of peace and beauty,' he decreed, greeting us warmly and offering us tea. It certainly sounded inviting, and this was a rather different reception from the one we were used to at Heathrow.

We were given two forms to complete but I found it impossible to write anything: the forms were in Arabic. That was reasonable – Arabic was the official national language – but the only Arabic I knew was a smattering of prayers and the Islamic greeting. For an entire hour, a customs official translated the forms for us haltingly, line by line, and interpreted our responses. As we left, he handed us city maps in assorted languages – none of which were English – to help us navigate our way around the country. We thanked him profusely.

Julian and I went exploring around the *souks* of Aleppo and bumped into the Grand Mosque, which opened out onto a large courtyard. The mosque staff strictly enforced the 'shoes-off' policy in the carpeted area: the mosque had to be clean because people were prostrating with their foreheads touching the same ground others had walked on. Our feet were expected to be cleaner than our shoes. It is true that our feet were easier to wash.[2]

Sunshine and warmth

I sat with Julian in the courtyard, enjoying the sunshine. Three men came up to us in turn, asking me to move to the ladies' prayer area. I understood why Muslim men and women stayed apart when in congregational prayer as we had to stand so closely that our shoulders and feet touched those of the person next to us. But I wasn't praying – I was simply absorbing the atmosphere. I stayed where I was.

A fourth man appeared and I wondered what he was going to say. 'Please, sit,' he insisted. 'I am so happy you are Muslim.' Julian's beard and my scarf had made our faith easy to spot. He proudly explained that this mosque housed the head of Zakariya, the guardian of Mary, mother of Jesus and a revered prophet in Islam. And then he told us he had to fetch something from his home. He returned within minutes, clutching a Qur'an, which he gave to us as a present.

Julian and I met other Syrians who were equally generous. When people saw we were Muslims travelling from abroad, they warmly invited us in to their homes. One man asked us to enter his building to take a shower: I had no idea I looked so dirty. And then I realized I had misunderstood his broken English – he wanted us to admire the 900-year-old Turkish baths he was renovating. We met entire extended families, we shared meals, we drank tea. And we gave them nothing except our thanks.

Socializing with the Syrians

We spent hours sitting in the otherwise all-male cafés, drinking tea. Men who were more confident with their English stopped playing cards, and engaged us in conversation. They were very concerned by the Syrian news reports about what was going on in England. 'What's it like having the Mafia there?' one asked. 'Do all English people have guns?' asked another. I tried to reassure them that England was quite safe. They laughed when I explained that English people thought it was Syria that was dangerous.

One man wanted to be certain that I was a 'proper' Muslim. 'Do you know *Surah Ikhlaas*?' he quizzed me, referring to the 112th chapter of the Qur'an. According to a *hadith*, it is equivalent in its meaning to a third of the entire Qur'an.[3] I recited the short chapter for him in Arabic, adding the English translation for good measure: 'Say He is the One God: God the Eternal, the Uncaused Cause of All Being. He begets not, and neither is He begotten; and there is nothing that could be compared with Him' (112:1–4). My new-found tea companion was triumphant. 'You see you don't know it,' he said.

He proceeded to translate it slowly, to educate me: 'Say He is One, He never dies. He doesn't have any babies and He has no mummy or daddy. And there is no one at all like Him.' I thought that was approximately what I said. But he couldn't see the connection.

I felt sorry for the Syrian women whom I presumed were sitting at home being oppressed. And then I met three ladies who told me otherwise. The women explained that the typical Syrian home was a hotbed of social activity for women, whose friends, neighbours and family would drop by for breakfast, lunch, dinner or any occasion in-between. One assured me that she was having a lot more fun than her card-playing husband. My father had always taught me never to assume anything: as usual, he had a point.

Just outside Aleppo, we visited St Simeon's monastery, where a Christian man had sat on a 15 metre high pillar for 42 years, preaching from on high. He made it his policy never to talk to women. I don't know why he was so fussy but, if that was his attitude, I probably wouldn't have wanted to talk to him either.

The road to Damascus

We then took a crowded mini-bus to Damascus and headed off to see the Christian part of the City, where shops sold pictures of a very Syrian-looking Virgin Mary with her equally Syrian-looking baby Jesus. I knew not one Muslim would buy the pictures – Jesus was considered to be a great Prophet in Islam, and Muslims would not depict any of their Prophets, just to make sure they were not inadvertently worshipped. Nevertheless, the Christian shops clearly wanted to appeal to Muslim customers and so stocked Qur'anic calligraphy alongside all the mother-and-baby pictures.

Julian and I came across an Orthodox Christian church service, which was being attended by a coach-load of Italian pilgrims. We were used to church services from our school days. But this one was different: there were images of saints wearing halos on the walls and the priest spent the entire service hidden behind a curtain.

The Italians then went on to see the house of Ananias; we followed and Julian used his smattering of Italian to listen in to what the tour guide was saying. The guide explained that Ananias was known for having cured Paul of his blindness. Paul was a critical figure in Christianity: Paul had received the gospel 'by the revelation of Jesus'[4] although he had never met Jesus himself. Paul had been blinded on the road to Damascus as light from heaven shone around him;[5] Ananias had restored his sight. Paul subsequently began preaching about the way Christians should live their life. The pilgrims began to pray at the site; we left them so they could be in private.

Alone in the desert

From Damascus, we caught a bus to Amaan in Jordan. Customs checks were straightforward on arrival: Julian was frisked, while I simply had my passport checked on the bus. We were both asked if we were carrying hashish, heroin or a video camera – it wasn't clear if they were all considered equally dangerous.

Amaan was in great contrast to Damascus, with a straightforward banking system, working streetlamps, tree-lined roads and women working everywhere we looked.

Julian and I checked into a budget hotel, where we bumped into two Austrian students whom we had previously encountered looking distressed on a bench in Aleppo in Syria, having just lost their only guidebook to the area. The four of us decided to share the cost of car hire so we could explore Wadi Rum, a vast desertscape of sand and rocks, over 300 km south of Amaan.

It was a miracle we ever made it out of Amaan given that I was map reading: our map was in English and all the signs were in Arabic. A policeman stopped us on the Desert Highway – once he established we were foreigners, he simply said 'have a nice day' and waved us on.

After walking for a mere 10 minutes through the desert in the blazing heat, we felt truly alone in the world. We stopped under a small tree to appreciate the scenery and the overwhelming sense of calmness. The peace was soon shattered.

A jeep roared up and a man brandishing a microphone jumped out. In a perfect English accent, he uttered the unforgettable phrase: 'We're from the BBC.' The reporter was eager to find out about our life-changing experiences in the desert. Given the small length of time we had been in the Wadi, we felt it only fair to suggest he should find some rather more seasoned explorers. Surrounded by sand dunes, we then received a quick run-down of the current English news – as well as the English weather.

Separated from the rest

From Jordan, we headed towards the West Bank, via the border crossing at Allenby Bridge. The crossing was less than 10 metres long but we had been warned that the journey could take hours, depending on the traveller's nationality. We Westerners were the lucky ones: after leaving the 'foreigners' terminal', we joined the 'foreigners' minibus', which sped through the border controls. We briefly caught sight of buses full of Palestinians waiting to go in the opposite direction.

Once we had arrived, Julian and I were separated from the other tourists: we had been identified as Muslim. We were put into individual cubicles each with our own armed Israeli soldier, who body searched us and asked us questions. Why were we visiting? Where had we come from? Where were we going? And who did we know in Israel and in Jordan? We emerged to find our cotravellers waiting patiently but with curiosity, wondering what we had done wrong. The security guard checking our rucksacks was much friendlier: she just asked me why I would voluntarily become Muslim and then broke the rules to allow me to hold on to my Jordanian honey – although she did tell me I had to keep it

We were able to travel quickly and easily throu
with the help of a taxi driver. The area wasn't large,
long by 48 km wide. It would be much more diffic
United Nations has counted over 540 Israeli road...

are manned checkpoints, positioned within this small section of the
Holy Land.[6] Then there is the 700 km security barrier, just over half of
which has been completed, severely restricting access both to many
villages within the West Bank, and from the West Bank to Jerusalem.[7]
But this was 1992: access was straightforward.

Holy sites

In Jericho, Julian and I stumbled and climbed our way up the Mount
of Temptation where, according to Biblical tradition, Jesus prayed
and fasted for 40 days and nights while being tempted by the Devil.[8]
We also visited an old Jewish synagogue, and dropped in at Elisha's
spring – Elisha being another Prophet common to Muslims,
Christians and Jews. Not unreasonably, at the spring we expected
to find some water. There wasn't any: it had all been diverted to
refugee camps for the Palestinians.

An Arab bus took us quickly on to Jerusalem. Two years before I
had visited Jerusalem as a Western tourist; now I was visiting as a
Western tourist who was also Muslim. Wherever we were, the Muslim
shop-owners engaged us in conversations about the political
situation. They also ensured we drank endless cups of tea.

We arrived at the area of Jerusalem known to Muslims as al-Haram
al Sharif and to Jews and Christians as 'Temple Mount'. This was the
site of Al Aqsa mosque, the third holiest mosque in Islam. But it was
after official tourist visiting hours: the Israeli security guard told us it
was closed. Julian explained that we were Muslim and we wanted to
pray. The guard accepted Julian was Muslim but needed convincing
about me: he told me to recite *Surah Fatihah* in Arabic to prove that I

⌣. I did; the guard allowed me to enter.

The Night Journey

Right next to Al Aqsa mosque was the photogenic Dome of the Rock, a mosque that was constructed to commemorate Muhammad's Night Journey, mentioned in the Qur'an (17:1). According to the more detailed *hadith*, Muhammad – accompanied by Angel Gabriel – was transported to Solomon's Temple, where he led a congregation of many of the earlier prophets in prayer. He then ascended with Gabriel into the heavens, encountering some of those prophets again: Adam, Jesus, John the Baptist, Joseph, Enoch, Aaron, Moses and Abraham.[9] When Muhammad reached the seventh heaven, God revealed to him that 50 prayers were now obligatory every day. Muhammad returned to Moses, who urged him to appeal for a reduction and God reduced the prayers by five. Muhammad went back and forth to Moses for further advice and upon hearing Muhammad's appeals, each time God reduced the number, finally bringing down the obligatory number of daily prayers to five.

I knew from reading Julian's wedding gift to me that the majority of Muhammad's companions believed these events physically happened, while some – including his wife Ayesha – were convinced that the Night Journey was purely spiritual in nature.[10] Neither view detracted from its significance, showing Islam as a continuation of the same message preached by earlier prophets. From that day on, Muslims were required as a symbol of their faith to pray five times a day. I was very grateful that I didn't have to fit in an extra 45.

Showing respect

As we stepped out of the mosque, a man sitting on the steps spoke to Julian. 'Please tell your wife her clothes should be longer,' he said. I was furious and took it out on Julian. 'Can't he see I am making an effort with these loose culottes? I am doing my best. And if he has a problem with me, why is he talking to you about it?' Julian assured me this man was trying be respectful by not talking to me directly and that he was only trying to be one of those mentioned in the Qur'an who 'enjoin the doing of what is right and forbid the doing of what is wrong' (3:104). His intentions may have been honourable, but I would have preferred it if he had kept quiet.

Just five minutes later, both of us were being reprimanded. As we walked around the grounds, a Palestinian security guard came up to us: 'No kiss, no touch, no hold hands,' he said in an agitated voice. 'No kiss, no touch, no hold hands.' We immediately stopped our unintentionally lewd behaviour – we had been holding hands.

The next day, we joined a guided tour for Westerners around Solomon's Temple. Our Israeli tour guide presented the complex history of Jerusalem in an understandable and appealing way. But then he decided it was relevant to explain the birth of Islam. 'Some guy picked bits from Judaism and Christianity to persuade the Pagans to stop fighting. It didn't go down very well so he tried it out on some others.' The guide was referring to Muhammad's initial experience in Mecca, where Muslims believe Muhammad received the revelation. He was joined by a small band of followers but they all suffered from both physical abuse and an economic boycott. Eventually Muhammad and his followers moved to Medina, where they were welcomed; many more accepted Islam. The tourists listened intently to the guide's rather more succinct description.

I couldn't stop myself from questioning the guide. 'How can you be sure that Muhammad took stories from the Bible?' I asked him. The guide retorted: 'Trust me, I'm the guide.' Muhammad couldn't read or write; the Christian monk Bahira whom Muhammad came across as a child already recognized the signs of his Prophethood; and another Christian called Waraqa helped to reassure Muhammad when he received his first revelation.[11] I responded: 'Yes, but many of the Qur'anic stories are slightly different to the Biblical version.

According to the Qur'an, Adam and Eve ate the fruit of the tree together;[12] it wasn't Eve who tempted Adam.' While the other tourists watched this exchange, the guide clearly didn't want it to continue: he moved us all on to the next part of the Temple. I was disappointed: we were on a site that was of such special significance to Jews, Christians and Muslims; it should have been the perfect opportunity to foster a bit of mutual understanding.

Our land

Our last sightseeing stop in Jerusalem was the Church of the Holy Sepulchre, which was run by several different Christian denominations, each responsible for their own sections of the church. One group showed us the site within their section where Jesus was buried; we then walked over to the next group who also showed us their site where Jesus was buried. Could they really both be right? It did seem a little unlikely.

That night we had dinner in a shopping mall outside Jerusalem's Old City. We ended up sitting next to a group of men: one was an Australian musician who was growing his ringlets in the style of an Orthodox Jew; one was an American enjoying a holiday he had dreamed of for years, and one was a Frenchman who had just become an Israeli citizen. They all agreed that this was their 'homeland'.

By bus, taxi, and aeroplane, we began the long journey back to our home.

Over to Indonesia

Once Julian and I had both graduated and enjoyed our 'official' wedding, we embarked on a backpacking honeymoon around Indonesia, home to the largest population of Muslims in the world.

We started off in Java, where we were welcomed as Muslims. We received discounts on breakfast and accommodation, we were invited to meet the entire family of two hostels we had found and we were even put at the front of the bus queue. It was clear positive discrimination. As we walked, people asked us: 'Bosnia? Bosnia?' The Bosnians were in the news, they were the only white Muslims that the Indonesians knew about, and it must have seemed entirely logical that a Bosnian would escape the massacres by backpacking around the Indonesian islands. The next question was: 'Married? No baby?' I smiled and replied, 'Insha'Allah' – God Willing. They said 'Insha'Allah' too. But I was only 21: I didn't really want God to will any babies just yet.

Culture and tradition

We enjoyed a guided walk through the jungle near Pangandarang, along with some other Western tourists. Along the way, the guide, unprompted, felt the need to reassure our group. 'I am not a fanatic, I am a neutral Muslim,' he said. He went on to explain: a neutral Muslim worships graves and also believes in the Queen of the Sea, a figure who whisks away anyone who dares to venture into the sea, particularly anyone wearing green. I knew that grave worshipping was clearly prohibited in Islam – although I had never come across anyone before who was tempted to do it – and this green-loving Queen sounded like a local cultural myth. But although the guide did not add to my understanding of the Qur'an, he did have an impressive level of knowledge about monkeys, bats and stalactites.

At Borabodur, a guide took us around what he told us was the world's largest Buddhist *stupa* or temple. It was covered in bells: the base of the bell represented the beginning, an upside down bell symbolized enlightenment, whereas a pole at the top was meant to look like a walking stick and, by implication, represent ageing. Our guide encouraged us to touch Buddha's foot: this was supposed to bring good luck. We touched the foot – we didn't want to offend our guide. Right at the end of the tour, the guide told us he was Muslim.

We told him that we were too. He was happy to hear that and, after his shift, took us to pray with him in the mosque – conveniently located within the Buddhist temple grounds.

Julian and I took a ferry from Java to beautiful Bali. Bali was almost entirely Hindu but I couldn't find any similarity with the monotheistic beliefs of my Hindu university friend Sriya. I saw shrines outside people's houses, shrines along the side of quiet roads and shrines at busy junctions. There was often an empty throne available for the god or goddess, accompanied by offerings of rice and delicate arrangements of flowers. We visited the 'Mother temple' of Bali, set in among the ubiquitous rice paddies – and we were only allowed out once we had made a donation to the gods.

The two of us moved on to the quieter and smaller neighbouring island of Lombok, where we began to encounter Muslims again, living alongside their Hindu neighbours. We met 'Mo' loitering by the boats. 'My full name is Mohammad' he explained when he saw us, but everyone calls me Mo. I'm a Muslim like you.' He had waist-length hair, skimpy shorts, and had his arms wrapped around two Western tourists. He went on to ask me: 'How am I meant to know you are female if you cover your hair with a scarf?' I felt such a comment didn't deserve an intelligent response and couldn't resist retorting: 'And how am I meant to know you are male when you are showing me such long hair?' He just laughed and turned his attention back to his girlfriends.

Places of worship

Julian and I rented a car to drive along the 'Trans-Lombok highway' and explore Lombok's interior. We were able to visit another temple in Lingsar: this one had a Muslim half and a Hindu half. The curator there used three hard-boiled eggs to entice a couple of massive 'sanctified' eels out from their hiding place in the pool located in the grounds – I was disappointed he never told us which religion had made them so sanctified. We went on to pray in a small mosque in the mountain town of Tetebatu; when we emerged, we were surrounded by dozens of villagers who had been peering through the windows. 'Bosnia?' asked one.

Julian and I caught a succession of ferries and buses to travel back though Java and on to Sumatra. There, we visited the picturesque mountain town of Bukittinggi. We saw young boys living – and sleeping – in the mosque: they were there to learn the art of eloquence. I tried unsuccessfully to imagine that happening in British mosques. A marching band of schoolgirls dressed in colourful Islamic school uniforms passed by: they were celebrating the 15 students who had just finished reading the Qur'an. We also attended a Muslim dance show where women in full length dresses and scarves performed various gentle and intricate moves involving coconuts – and then demonstrated some less gentle self-defence techniques using knives.

One restaurant owner was very pleased to see us as his restaurant didn't receive many tourists – unlike the other Muslim-owned restaurants in the area, he kept his premises alcohol free. He explained that the Islamic culture in the town here was strongly matriarchal so, upon marriage, the husband would often go to live with the wife's family. I was about to go and stay for a week with my husband's.

Women's issues

Our honeymoon ended in Saudi Arabia.

The two of us arrived in Dhahran, in the Eastern Province of Saudi Arabia, where we walked down the tarmac road to the internal terminal. We had our heavy rucksacks on our back; we were both wearing trousers and loose tops and I had a white scarf. I couldn't help noticing the bemused stares from the Saudi men, all dressed in long white tunics. The women were dressed from head to toe in black, with their faces covered, so I couldn't tell if they were looking too.

We flew on to the capital of Saudi Arabia, Riyadh, to visit Julian's mother Nagila and her Italian Muslim husband Gianni who were expatriates in the country. Gianni explained that it was a legal requirement for me to wear a floor-length black cloak or *abaya* over whatever I was wearing but, because I wasn't Saudi, I didn't have to cover my face and I could wear a headscarf that was not black. The white garments, known as *thobes*, were reserved for men. This was the Saudi solution to the Islamic guidelines that men and women must be both modest and clearly distinguishable from the opposite sex. I strongly objected to being forced to wear the black *abaya* but I had no choice about complying: I was in their country and it was the law.

Nagila showed me her extensive collection of cloaks, which ranged from plain black to ornately decorated – albeit still black. When I went out, I wore my 'normal' clothes, but just spent a few extra seconds putting on the *abaya* as well. I discovered it wasn't such a big deal. Nevertheless, I still thought it was unnecessary and I didn't want to be told how to dress by a government. And I couldn't help associating the colour black with being oppressed.

Julian's mother wore black in public in Saudi Arabia but was far from oppressed. She was a counsellor and taught porcelain painting, practising both skills from home. She even presented her own television programme. Although legally prohibited from driving herself, my mother-in-law had a dedicated driver and so managed to have full mobility without the stress of driving on the roads of Riyadh. She also had a full-time maid and a cook. It seemed a pretty good life to me even if she did have to wear black.

Thank God it's Thursday

Then Julian and I were introduced to Khalil, a young Saudi friend of the family who had kindly agreed to show us around for a few days. At the home of my in-laws, I dutifully served tea to Khalil and his friends but didn't get any acknowledgement. It was as if I wasn't there. Khalil was studying medicine and showed Julian his medical textbook where he had conscientiously folded over every page that displayed the female anatomy. Julian explained to me that Khalil was being respectful: I had never seen respect being shown like this before. Khalil was desperate to call Julian by an Arabic name and kept asking him to suggest one. Once he discovered Julian's middle name was Hamish, he began to refer to Julian as 'Khamis' – with a silent 'k': it was an Arabic name meaning Thursday.

As we drove through Riyadh, past the segregated restaurants and segregated theme parks, Khalil said to Julian: 'Khamis, your wife may ask me questions if she wants.' I didn't. We were at the shops when the *adhan* went, calling all the Muslims to prayer. The shops shut, the male shopkeepers left to pray and the men in the shops went with them. I waited outside with other women: the mosque nearby was only for men. I was unable to perform my obligatory prayer in this country ruled by Islam.

I left Saudi Arabia feeling very negative about being Muslim. If this was Islam, I wasn't impressed. But of course it wasn't Islam: as the speaker in the Islamic Foundation had reminded me, Islam was 'a forty-lane highway'. These Saudis and I were just in very different lanes.

A relative welcome

From Riyadh, we were flying on to Sharjah, in the United Arab Emirates. Our flight wouldn't be leaving to the UK until the following day, and we hadn't got around to organizing any accommodation.

Just before we left Riyadh, my mother-in-law mentioned to us that she had a relative living in Sharjah. Nagila couldn't describe exactly how Julian was related to him, but did know he was some kind of 'uncle'. Julian had never met him before. Julian called him from a phone booth on arriving at Sharjah airport, and engaged in a few minutes of small talk before mentioning that we happened to be around the corner.

The uncle insisted we must stay with him and his family: within 20 minutes, he was at the airport to pick us up. We ate dinner on his living room floor with our hands, in keeping with polite Arab tradition. I tried to be discreet about the mess I was making. The uncle then spent the evening driving us around local sights and introducing us to other relatives whom we didn't know. At night time, he gave up the main bedroom for us while he slept with his wife on the living room floor. The following morning, he escorted us to the airport and spoke to one of his friends who worked there. Our luggage – and then our seats – were instantly upgraded, from economy class to business class. I was overwhelmed: this relative had never met Julian before and had certainly never heard of me but he had gone out of his way to make us feel welcome.

We arrived at Heathrow to find Jeffery waiting in Arrivals, together with five other Muslim friends. *'Assalamu Alaikum,'* Jeffrey called out, using the universal Muslim greeting of peace, as he spotted us with our luggage.

The holiday was definitely over. I was about to join the ranks of the British labour force.

4 In the 'Real World'

'Men shall have a benefit from what they earn, and women shall have a benefit from what they earn.'

(Qur'an 4:32)

'To try to earn a lawful livelihood is an obligation like the other obligations in Islam.'

(Saying of Muhammad).

I was looking forward to working.

Through home and school, I had been brought up to aspire to a career. My girls' school had taught us that women could have a career that was at least as good as a man's – and ideally better. But more recently, I had read books about Islam, which explained that, upon marriage, a Muslim man must take full economic responsibility for his wife. It sounded like someone had been talking to my father.

I knew that as a Muslim woman I had the right to work. Women always worked during Muhammad's lifetime. Muhammad's wife Khadijah was a highly successful businesswoman; she was also his boss and even instigated the marriage proposal.[1] She was not alone in working during that time: women owned fields and date-palm orchards, women traded in the markets, women engaged in arts and crafts, and women gave medical care to those wounded on the battlefield. Some were even doing the fighting themselves.[2] I preferred to have an office job.

A fledgling career

In the interview for my first graduate job, as a financial analyst in a multinational consumer goods company, the financial director was giving me a hard time. 'You've told me your father went to a good university and he has worked for years in this same line of business. I see you've also come from a good university. What an easy life.' And he continued: 'What makes you so special? When have you ever done anything unexpected?'

I said the only thing that popped into my head. 'Well, I've become Muslim', I proffered. I knew the last thing you should mention in a job interview is religion. I think he knew it too. That line of questioning came to an abrupt end. Two days later I heard that I had got the job: whether it was despite this response or because of it, I'll never know.

I was excited at the thought of earning a salary. According to Islam, I could keep it all for myself if I wanted – although the downside would be that we would then be unable to pay the bills. And so we agreed to put both our pay cheques into a joint bank account and watched the money flow out again almost immediately to cover rail tickets, the rental deposit, the rent, the gas, the electricity and the telephone. It wasn't as much fun being grown-up as I had imagined.

On the day of my first assignment, in the oral care industry, I arrived at the UK headquarters feeling nervous. Not only was I about to learn about a new world of toothpaste and toothbrushes – I was also now wearing the headscarf, which I hadn't been wearing at the time of the interview.

I was introduced to my boss, who was Scottish. 'I love my beer, and I don't care for religion,' he told me. At least I knew where I stood.

A place to pray

In our very initial meeting, I asked my boss where I could pray. I thought if I could get that issue out of the way, we could move on to discuss the toothpaste and toothbrush range that I was being paid to analyse. 'I don't need anything special', I explained. 'Just a small place where no-one will come in for five minutes.' He was initially stumped, before suggesting the Sick Room.

The Head of Human Resources told me: 'You are welcome to use the Sick Room, but if there ever is someone who is sick and needs to rest, that person will have to take priority.' That seemed fair. 'Of course,' I agreed. From that day on, the Sick Room had two functions; fortunately few people at work seemed to get sick.

And then one lunchtime, I found the Sick Room occupied. I had to find somewhere else to pray, and I could see the Finance Director's office was empty. I asked his secretary if I could take over his room for five minutes. 'No problem,' she assured me. 'He's in a meeting; he won't be back for ages.' I had just started the prayer when he popped in to get something: he found me bending down and then putting my forehead on his carpet. He asked me several questions but I was praying: I couldn't speak to anyone, including a Finance Director. I ignored him, trying unsuccessfully to concentrate. My heart sank when I saw him again as I came out of his office but he simply said, 'hello'. 'Hello,' I replied, and walked quickly back to my desk.

My fasting cousin

A Jewish marketing colleague who was also immersed in toothpaste matters came up to me, and asked where I went to pray. David explained that it was Yom Kippur, the time of a Jewish 24-hour fast and he wanted to mark the occasion by praying as well as fasting. I was voluntarily fasting for the day too: it was the tenth of the lunar month known to Jews as *Tishrei* and known to Muslims as *Ashura*. We were both commemorating events relating to Moses.

When David came back from praying, the two of us talked about our 'same but different' experiences of praying, fasting and traditional customs. We had so much in common. It wasn't surprising: not only did we share the story of Moses – we accepted that a central forefather in each of our faiths was Abraham. Muhammad was a descendant of Abraham's son Ismail, known in Arabic as Ishmael, and Moses was a descendant of his other son Isaac, or Ishaq. We joked we were cousins; we were both careful not to let modern-day politics ruin our relationship.

The conversation provided a temporary distraction from the economics of oral hygiene, the more typical reason for our interactions.

Suspecting the men

I commuted every day to my workplace from the basement flat we were renting in Putney in London. Julian and I had quickly got into a routine.

Then in November, just two months after we had started work, I returned home to find the door locked and chained from the inside. I rang the bell. Julian had arrived two minutes before me and now called out to me. 'Climb through the kitchen window,' he shouted. I squeezed through, wondering what he was playing at. He wasn't laughing: we had been burgled and it was the burglars who had chained the door.

Julian and I checked out the damage. The burglars had found one of our large kitchen knives, and left it lying on the dresser. Then they had helped themselves to all my wedding jewellery and to my Christening presents that my mother had looked after for 21 years – and that I had looked after for a couple of months. They had also defecated throughout the flat, including on my clothes, which they had pulled out from the drawers.

'Men on drugs,' diagnosed the police confidently, when they came around to inspect the scene. 'There has been a spate of burglaries up this road in the last few months.' A policeman explained it wasn't worth spending the time and paperwork required to find and arrest the perpetrators because, even if they were caught, they would be out of jail within months. The burglars didn't have much of a deterrent to prevent them from doing it again.

For several months afterwards, as I walked up and down Putney High Street, I was suspicious of every man I passed. I wondered if he had been involved in ransacking our flat. It was an irrational reaction but I felt the need to direct my fears somewhere.

At the time, I was reading a book by Akbar Ahmed, described by the BBC as 'probably the world's best-known scholar on contemporary Islam.'[3] He was documenting a general and growing suspicion directed towards all Muslims. Suspicion of Muslims was growing after the 'Muslim' book-burning of *The Satanic Verses*, after the corruption scandal in the 'Muslim' bank BCCI and after the illegal invasion of Kuwait by a dictator who called himself Muslim. I wasn't the only one with generalized fears.

We didn't get burgled again. In Putney High Street, I started trusting the men.

A foreign body

The men at work – and the women – assumed I had become Muslim because of a man. Once they established I was Muslim, the next two questions were predictable. 'So who's your husband then? Where does he come from?'

'He's from Chertsey,' I replied. The hospital where he was born was less than 8 km from the office. It was 20 km from where I was born. We had gone to primary schools over the road from each other. As a young child, he used to come weekly along with his boys' school to use the swimming pool of my girls' school – he occasionally peeped through the windows to see the girls swimming. I used to see those boys at the window: I had no idea I might eventually marry one of them.

The questioners persisted. 'But where's he really from?' I persisted too: Julian was from Chertsey. But then I gave in to what they wanted to hear. I told them that he was half-Iranian. Around 150 years ago his ancestors on his mother's side had come from Iran. But Julian had been born and brought up in England. Julian wasn't foreign and I wasn't Muslim because of him. I would never change my beliefs for any man – or any woman.

I soon discovered it wasn't only work colleagues who thought I was Muslim because I was married to one. I joined my old university friend, Adi, for an evening meal after work – Adi and I had often had tea together while I was in the process of becoming Muslim. At the open-air restaurant, I hesitated for a second deciding what drink I was going to have. Adi was quick to tell me: 'Julian isn't around, you know, you can order what you want.' I did: I ordered apple juice.

But being married to a Muslim did make it easier for me to be one, particularly given that I was surrounded for most of the time by those who weren't. It helped to be living with someone who didn't think I was completely mad. At the weekends, we prayed most of the prayers together. He was also particularly good at making pasta.

Like all couples without domestic help, Julian and I needed to agree who would do what around the house. It was not a difficult decision: we both cleaned, I washed dishes and clothes and he cooked. Julian's mother found it a bit of a culture shock that her son was often in the kitchen but she soon saw that this division of labour was in everybody's interests. As my father had fondly relayed to our wedding guests, I had even failed my Brownie cookery badge. Anyway, Julian wasn't doing anything Islamically unusual: Muhammad had helped with the housework and stitched his own clothes. He had even mended his own shoes – although both Julian and I preferred to go to the repair shop around the corner.

Free to marry

I discovered another Muslim at work. Her name was Atya, she worked full time and she was born in the UK. Atya lived with her Pakistani parents; she was firmly single. We began to pray together in the Sick Room and discussed our lives on the way to and from our desks.

Then one day Atya approached my desk holding a photograph: 'This is the man I'm going to marry,' she announced happily. I was shocked: where had he suddenly come from? She explained. 'Kamran is a distant relative of mine who lives in Pakistan; I've never met him but my father knows his family really well. And I trust my father to make the right decision. I'm only going to meet him on the day of the wedding.' I couldn't believe that my 'modern' friend was happy with that plan: to me it sounded like a living nightmare. But she was very excited at the prospect; she had always expected an arranged marriage.

I knew other Muslims who had experienced arranged marriages, although they had all known their spouse rather better beforehand. Several girls had got married after initially being introduced to a succession of men through their parents: each man had come to the girl's home for a formal tea and chat with the prospective bride and her family. If they both liked what they saw, they talked again – on the telephone or through email – and met up, either out in public or at home with family. The couple was not meant to be alone until they were married, just in case that third person 'temptation' appeared too. These marriages cemented family ties and ensured that connections were made between 'good' families. The stories reminded me of the novels I had read set in Victorian times. I had tried to match up people myself, but it never led to anything: one relationship looked promising until the girl told me she simply didn't like the way the man sat.

Know your partner

I had met Muslim couples who had found their soulmate themselves – some through university, others through work or community projects. There were those who had met at a wedding, where marriage was an obvious topic of conversation. One friend of mine found her spouse on-line, through an Islamic chat room. Times were changing fast.

I didn't know any woman who had experienced a forced marriage, a marriage where they had been 'married off' without their permission. I knew it happened – the media reported it. But within Islam, a marriage was only valid if both partners in their relationship had given their permission.[4] In Muhammad's lifetime, he used to annul a forced marriage or give both spouses the option of ending it. Forced marriages were nothing to do with Islam.

Atya went off to Pakistan to have her arranged marriage. When she returned, I visited her home and watched the wedding video. Atya recounted the first embarrassing moments that they were left alone together and told me how sad she felt leaving her new husband. She had to leave Kamran behind since the British Consulate in Karachi first needed to interview him. At the interview, they asked her husband lots of questions. What's Atya's favourite food? Where did she go to school? Who lives next door? He didn't know. Of course he didn't: he hardly knew her. But fortunately, the Consulate believed them when they each separately explained the marriage was legitimate. After the first four months of marriage spent in different continents, Atya's husband was allowed to join her in England.

Hot and cold

I caught up with the latest developments in Atya's life at the office restaurant. As usual, I turned up wearing a scarf while Atya didn't. Atya also told the canteen staff she was a vegetarian. 'You are both

Muslim,' said a confused colleague standing next to us in the queue. 'Why aren't you both the same?'

During the queues at the canteen – and over lunch – work colleagues asked me a whole series of questions about the scarf. 'Why do Muslims wear it anyway?' 'Is it a symbol of your religion?' Is it a political statement?' 'Why is it women who have to do all the covering up?' 'Does your husband make you wear it?' 'Jemima Khan doesn't wear it, so why do you?' Then there were more: 'How can I see your facial expression if I can't see your entire forehead?' 'Do you wear it in the shower?' 'Do you wear it in front of your husband?' 'Does a baby have to wear it?' 'You're so lucky – does that mean you never have to wash your hair?' I was asked 'Are you cold?' but more often: 'Don't you get hot?'

I had a lot of explaining to do. I explained that the reason for wearing it was practical rather than symbolic or political: the scarf was simply a small but visible contribution to the idea of Muslim modesty in behaviour and dress. I told them I didn't wear it in front of other women and I didn't wear it in front of my husband: I only wore it in front of men of marriageable age to whom I was not related. A couple of male colleagues felt personally offended.

I clarified that I didn't need to wear the scarf in the shower and so could wash my hair as often – or as infrequently – as I wanted. Like one of my questioners, I also searched the whole of people's faces for expression, including their forehead – and I was happy for people to look at mine. None of the Islamic recommendations applied until puberty: I mentioned I had seen one baby with a scarf on but it was freezing cold at the time and the mother was simply trying to keeping her baby warm. Yes, sometimes the scarf helped when it was cold. And when it was warm, I switched to wearing a light white version. On the 'plus' side, I had less need for either an umbrella or a sun hat. I had never met Jemima Khan: my decision was my own.

Standing out

People outside my workplace also wondered about my hair covering. I was taking management accountancy exams and had been awarded extra time due to a computer-related arm injury. After my morning exam the external invigilator came up to me deeply concerned about the reason for my extra time. He asked me about my brain cancer. Motioning towards my head, I explained that I only wore the scarf because I was Muslim. Unfortunately, he wasn't that relieved: he told me he was Christian. Specifically, he was an evangelical Christian: he decided I needed educating about the true nature of Jesus. I was desperate to revise for my afternoon exam on product costing and extricated myself from his monologue as soon as I could. A fellow passenger on my commuter train back home asked me 'What order do you belong to?' He thought I was from a convent.

I had chosen to wear the scarf for modesty reasons. I didn't mean to advertise my Muslimness to people around me; it was just one of the consequences. When I was out with my grandmother, I tried to make my scarf slightly less obvious to make her feel more comfortable. I tied it under my neck the way older ladies used to. Granny was up front in her reaction. 'The scarf looks nice on you, Lucy, but I prefer it when you wear it the other way.' I was touched by her compliment but surprised that she had any kind of scarf-tying preference. 'What other way?' I asked her. 'You know, when you wear it with the ends flicked over your shoulders' she replied straightaway. I stopped attempting to blend in and reverted back to my usual ways.

Atya only wore a scarf when she was praying. 'I wasn't brought up to wear it,' she explained. She went on to tell me how wearing a scarf was looked down upon by many middle-class girls in Pakistan, both as a sign of poverty and lack of education.

I now knew lots of other Muslims outside my workplace: some covered their hair and others didn't. These women who didn't had different reasons for not wearing it. Some weren't sure it was a necessary part of the faith. One was experiencing severe opposition from her Muslim husband. Others genuinely wanted to but didn't want to cope with the reactions of other people. Several English Muslim converts preferred their faith to remain rather less visible.

I did cover my hair – it was a 10-second addition to my daily dressing routine. But I was very aware that it didn't make me a 'better' Muslim than those who didn't. God would be judging each member of humanity on their inner faith and their outward actions; wearing that scarf was just one action out of many.

The meat-eating vegetarian

Eating meat from animals which had been cared for both in life and during death was another.

Certain meat was declared in the Qur'an to be *haram* – forbidden – including pork, and animals killed by strangling, and animals killed in a name other than God's (5:3). And anything that was not forbidden was *halal*, or permissible.

Like the majority of Muslims, Atya did eat meat, but only from animals that that had been killed in a certain way. Muslims slaughter animals using the *zabihah* method: saying '*Bismillah*' – 'in the name of God' – as they kill each animal; using only healthy livestock; ensuring that other animals don't see it dying; employing a sharp knife to the neck to ensure a quick death and, finally, letting the blood drain. Atya and I – like all other Muslims – knew when this had been carried out fully, as there would be a notice in the butcher's shop, the restaurant, or indeed the canteen, declaring the meat *halal*. And if there was no such declaration, then in public Atya chose to say she was vegetarian: she found it so much easier. I could see our colleague was frowning but he said he understood.

Permissible business

I took a short business flight to Brussels and read the in-flight menu, which said that that the snack being offered included bacon. And so I asked if there was a spare *kosher* meal, since any meat that was *kosher* for the Jews would not only be bacon-free but would also have been killed in a way comparable to the Muslim *zabihah* process – albeit with various additional injunctions being followed. I felt very self-conscious when my food arrived: while those around me received a small bacon croissant, I was given a three-course meal with a notice declaring that a rabbi had blessed it.

At the time, I was working on a business idea, for *halal* toothpaste. Any product could be certified *halal* as long as it contained neither alcohol nor any non-*halal* animal products. The idea grew: I believed enough Muslims would love it to make it commercially viable. My manager agreed that I should look into it; I discussed the idea with the European factory. My contact in production did his research, before telling me that it would be impossible to ensure current production methods complied with the requirements. Our main competitor was already producing *halal* toothpaste in other countries – although consumers would never know unless they asked – but we were not going to be making it yet. I redirected my energy towards the general market for mouthwash, working hard before the holiday season began.

Jingle bells

It was nearly Christmas at the office: it was time for the Secret Santa. We each pulled a name out of the hat and had to buy a low-value item for the named colleague. Then, on the last day in the office before the holidays, we took turns unwrapping the anonymous gift sitting in front of us. I had bought an incredibly intelligent colleague a family of rubber ducks for the bath. I opened my present –

everyone else found it hilarious. It featured 'the Chippendales', the provocative male dancers, starring in a nude pin-up calendar. I couldn't see myself displaying that on my desk. The two other female financial analysts began to discuss which of them would take it if I didn't want it: it disappeared within minutes.

The office Christmas party was imminent. My colleagues asked me to be their minibus driver for the evening. To them, it made perfect sense: they could drink as much alcohol as they wanted, and I would remain sober. But for me, the thought of driving around London in the early hours of the morning while they were potentially vomiting in the back seat just didn't appeal. I turned down their offer.

But I did become popular around Christmas due to the annual Christmas hamper. Each of us received a massive box filled with luxury food items: chocolates, expensive jams, selections of biscuits and bottles of wine. I took my box to Reception: the area filled up with people wanting to exchange their packet of chocolate biscuits for my alcohol. I took home my hamper, now filled with chocolate.

And then I came across a *hadith* about alcohol, where I learnt that I was not only meant to stay away from drinking it, I was not meant to sell it either.[5] That was a shame: I had been selling mine, albeit not for money but for confectionery. So I changed. The next time, I took out what I liked and left all the alcoholic items in the hamper; I then put the box out with my household rubbish, ready for the refuse collectors. 'Aren't they the lucky ones?' said my mother.

Have an orange juice

The issue of alcohol was a minefield at work: there were just so many 'social drinking' occasions. 'Are you coming to the pub?' a colleague asked me as the department left for a quick drink after work at the end of a long week. 'You can always have an orange juice'. 'Are you coming to the pub?' asked another, as the department got together for a birthday celebration at lunchtime. 'Are you coming to the pub?' emailed a third, who was organizing his leaving drinks.

I knew that some Muslims happily watched their friends drinking in a pub or restaurant and that other Muslims drank alcohol themselves. According to Islam, Muslims are clearly not meant to drink or even – in one common interpretation – sit with people who were drinking. Yet we each make our own choices. While I maintain an alcohol-free home, I do sit with my family if they have wine on their table – there is an Islamic principle of weighing up 'competing priorities' and I strongly believe that strengthening the family relationships has to come first. But going to the pub with colleagues was not such a priority.

After three years, it was my turn to leave the company. 'Are we all going to the pub?' my colleagues asked.

Out of the closet

I moved on to a pharmaceutical company where I enjoyed the non-pub-related work and social activities – including a team-building dinner held at an exclusive restaurant in London. As I sat with my teetotal Bahai and Hindu workmates at one end of the table, the alcohol-fuelled conversation got increasingly loud at the other end. I decided to leave early. And then, as I was walking past the others and saying 'Good bye', one of my male marketing colleagues got out of his seat and gave me an unexpected and warm embrace.

As Ben hugged me, he seemed to be crying. I had no idea what was going on. In-between holding back tears, he explained. 'You and I have got so much in common. I've always respected you, Lucy: you've come out with what you believe in, in front of everyone and even in front of your parents. I've never felt able to do this.' But I finally realized he was talking about being gay – people in the department had wondered if he was.

And then Ben added: 'My parents still don't know.' I had previously assumed that, in England, declaring oneself to be gay would be so much more acceptable than telling people you were now a Muslim. In politics, business, and in the media world, homosexuals were 'coming out' all the time. But, it dawned on me that, whatever the public attitude was, for parents it was personal. At least if your child chose to be Muslim, you were more likely to end up with grandchildren – even if they were Muslim ones.

I got into the taxi back home, feeling bad that Ben had hugged me but happy that he had felt able to tell me what he was on his mind. Once we were back in the workplace, it was clear that Ben's outburst had been entirely drink related. In the restaurant, the alcohol had relaxed him enough to open up. In the office, he was sober. He never mentioned his lifestyle again.

Family values

Julian's family was so large that it encompassed many different approaches to life.

After the wedding, I had received genealogical lessons. Julian and his Aunty Lulu had counted everyone up using their fingers and concluded that he had 52 first cousins as well as half- and once-removed varieties. I only had five cousins, three of whom I sadly never saw. Many of his aunts and uncles had married outside their original community to people who were English, Italian, Australian, German, American and Mexican. The diversity looked set to carry on down the generations: Jeffery was planning to marry a Chinese convert to Islam. Her full name was Li-Jia – Li being her surname and Jia her first name. I wondered what the postman would make of that.

Jeffery always answered the telephone by saying 'Assalamu Alaikum', the traditional Muslim greeting meaning 'Peace be upon you.' When Jeffery came by to our flat, he suggested I try it too. I agreed to give it a go. Just a few minutes later, the phone rang. I picked it up, saying *'Assalamu Alaikum'*. 'What was that?' said the voice at the end of the phone. 'What did you say?' It was my father. 'Oh nothing,' I replied. I promptly reverted back to saying 'hello'.

Without exception, Julian's family was warm and welcoming. Aunts and uncles had already been generous with their wedding presents; now they invited us over and showered us with food and gifts to take away. Second cousins once removed invited me into their house and were open in conversation. I was happy to be part of such a big family and grew to love those I came to know. I couldn't manage to name all 52 first cousins though. Or was it 53?

A cousin questioned our 'Muslimness' when she caught us eating sweets that had not been officially certified as *halal*. She was worried that our Jelly Babies might contain non-*halal* animal gelatine. Julian explained that its original form had been altered so much through chemical processes that some said it didn't count as having animal origins any more. *Halal*-certification organizations were debating among themselves about whether the gelatine could be considered *halal*. We disagreed with Julian's cousin but that was fine: she had her views, we had ours.

But then the cousin went on to chat about her cannabis habit, which she was convinced was making her forget a lot of her schoolwork. She had also just been found passing cannabis to another student on the school grounds: suspension was now a real possibility. All mind-altering substances were clearly forbidden in Islam. Julian and I decided to stick with our Jelly Babies.

Changing the habit

Another member of the family – let's call him Tariq – was also having a difficult time with drugs: he had become hooked on cocaine, another mind-altering substance that was forbidden according to both Islamic and British law. Once we were sure he had a problem,

Tariq's brother brought him to our flat – it was the most convenient place for him to stay. He spent the first evening fully clothed in the bath. Julian was away at the time: it was just Tariq and me. Strictly speaking the two of us shouldn't have been sharing the flat without a third person present as we weren't closely related. But I knew that in Islam, extreme circumstances meant previously forbidden actions became allowed. If I was starving, I could eat pork. I figured that, by analogy, if I was the only one around to help, then I could live alone with an unrelated male drug addict.

I wasn't sure what to do, so I went to work. I returned to find Tariq calm; he had just been to Enfield in North London to receive his next fix. 'It's terrible, I spent last night looking around your place to see what I could steal,' he confessed. I was glad he had found another way to fund his habit for the day. I spent the evening on the telephone to drugs help lines to get some much-needed and non-judgemental advice and support.

I went back to work the next day but couldn't concentrate. I was worried about what was happening at home. So I went to see the Head of Human Resources to discuss the issue and ended up crying. She generously gave me three days off work to deal with the situation. And she made me a cup of tea.

I drove home and accompanied Tariq to a counselling session, where I sat in the waiting area along with a group of men. They were holding an animated discussion about how they were spending their children's benefits on drugs – and how fed up their partners were getting. Frustratingly for me, Tariq's counselling session was confidential: I had to rely on him to want to open up about the discussion. On the bus journey back, I asked Tariq about where he had obtained his drugs. I got more and more information. When I was on my own, I quietly attempted to give details of his drugs-dealer friend Eric to the people running the national drugs hotline. The drugs squad told me they already had their eye on Eric and were keen to get more evidence. Once again, I felt like I had entered a different world. But this was a world I had no wish to be in. Tariq's brother didn't want his mother to know, but I called her anyway. I couldn't handle the situation alone.

It was a relief when his brother and mother joined me. I knew the situation wasn't his mother's fault – or his father's. As I knew all too well, parents did their best and children chose their own path. But some paths were self-destructive. Between the three of us we physically barricaded Tariq into the flat for four days and managed to wean him off the drug. It required endless tough conversations, unconditional love and heartfelt personal and ritual prayers. Tariq finally appreciated his family would always be there for him, whatever happened – unlike some of his friends. For many months afterwards, he had to make a concerted effort to resist further temptation. But he managed. And now he doesn't even touch alcohol or cigarettes. Thank God for that. I went back to my 'normal life'.

Extremists at work

At work, security was being increased. Pharmaceutical companies with the slightest connection to animal testing for use in medical research were being targeted by animal rights activists. Three extremists had broken in to one of the chemistry labs, and destroyed expensive equipment. A director had been telephoned and threatened. 'We know where you live,' they had told him.

Our internal telephone directories were changed: they no longer revealed the position of each employee. We had to answer the telephone using our first names only. Additional security guards were employed at the entrance to the site; visitors had to be received at the entrance and escorted in by a member of the department that was expecting them. Children were no longer allowed to visit – although no one was suspecting them of extremist activity. Everybody was affected.

While the vast majority of animal lovers did not even engage in peaceful protest, let alone violent attacks, there was a small, vocal minority who were prepared to use force to make their point.

Extreme elements were found in many groups: animal rights activists were just one example. But the actions of a few had affected us all: we were all forced to modify our way of working during office hours.

Classes at the mosque

I had time in the evenings and weekends and thought I could use some of it to learn Arabic, the unchanged language of the Qur'an.

My first effort was a disaster. I went back to the Central Mosque in London, to the weekend *madrasa* – a supplementary school for Muslim children. A teacher asked for my level of Arabic knowledge. I explained: 'I'm an absolute beginner.' So she allocated me to the class for five-year-olds on the basis that we all knew as little Arabic as each other. But the children had a rather different learning style from me, spending most of the time colouring in pictures that started with different Arabic letters. I never did like colouring and was not about to start now. They also had tiny chairs.

I had a second attempt at that mosque, going to an adult evening class where I sat discreetly at the back. Unfortunately, the teacher soon spotted me and asked me to repeat the entire alphabet after him. The letter 'ha' completely stumped me – it was meant to come from my throat in a kind of breathless whisper but I clearly didn't do it properly. The well-intentioned teacher then spent a painful thirty minutes of the two-hour group class on correcting my Arabic pronunciation.

I had always struggled to correctly pronounce any language other than English. The episode brought back unhappy memories of my French oral tuition at aged 15 where, on one stressed-out occasion, I brought piping hot tea to my long-suffering teacher and then promptly spilt it all over him. I knew there was a *hadith* about how a person who recited the Qur'an with difficulty got twice the reward of the one who recited it perfectly.[6] I didn't mind having difficulty; and I didn't want to be the sole focus of a group lesson.

Attending the lesson were two other English female converts. One had come from Finsbury Park. After the lesson was over she explained she was very distressed. Her local mosque had just been taken over by someone who was only allowing his followers to pray there: his name was Abu Hamza. She was very frustrated with the police, who said they couldn't do anything to help.

Another girl was my age and lived just one train stop away from me: her name was Wendy. Wendy also wanted to learn Arabic and she organized a private tutor to come as a one-off to her home to teach the two of us. It was soon obvious that Wendy was way ahead of me: she already knew her alphabet. We stopped learning Arabic together and chatted over tea instead.

Reading the signs

But I still wanted to learn the language. I made a telephone call to an Arabic school outside London that offered weekend classes for adults. The Head of the school asked me what my job was. I was now a profit forecaster, so I told him my job title. There was a prolonged silence at the end of the phone and then he said to me, with disbelief clear in his voice, 'You forecast prophets?' I don't know how he thought I spent my time: Muslims believe we have had the last one. We seemed to be approaching life from rather different perspectives.

I endeavoured to try Arabic evening classes once again, attending the School of Oriental and African Studies in London. All my fellow students wanted to learn modern Arabic so they could speak it in conversation, rather than to read and understand the classical Arabic of the Qur'an. They found it unusual that, in Arabic, I could say 'In the name of God Most Gracious most Merciful' but found it hard to tell them what my name was or how many brothers and sisters I had.

It was 1997. After five-and-a-half years of being a Muslim I could manage to recite enough Arabic to do my prayers but, frustratingly, couldn't even read the occasional Arabic *halal* signs in UK restaurants, let alone the Qur'an in its original language. But that didn't stop me attempting to fulfil the different pillars of the faith, including going on the pilgrimage of *Hajj*.

5   A Pilgrim's Progress

'For, when We assigned unto Abraham the site of this Temple, [We said
unto him] "Do not ascribe divinity to aught beside Me!" – and: "Purify
My Temple for those who will walk around it, and those who will stand
before it [in meditation], and those who will bow down and prostrate
themselves [in prayer]." Hence, [O Muhammad,] proclaim thou unto all
people the [duty of] pilgrimage: they will come unto thee on foot and
on every [kind of] fast mount, from every far-away point [on earth], so
that they might experience much that shall be of benefit to them.'

(Qur'an 22:26–28)

'You must adhere to the traditions and rituals [of *Hajj*], for these have
come down to you from [your forefather] Abraham in heritage.'[1]

(Saying of Muhammad)

I knew I had to make the pilgrimage to Mecca once in my lifetime, to
complete the fifth pillar of Islam. It was 1997: Julian and I now had a
bit of money, a lot of energy, and no children – the three facts were
probably connected. And so Julian suggested, 'Why don't we go on
Hajj this year?' There was no reason not to (3:97).[2]

Closer to God?

Before becoming a Muslim, I had thought a pilgrimage was
something people went on in order to find a miraculous cure for

crippling ailments. I didn't want curing. I wanted to go to fulfil an obligation decreed by God, an obligation that would bring together people from all races, cultures, classes and regions, to one place, to worship one God. The pilgrimage to Mecca was a ritual performed since the time of Abraham – and by Muhammad 1,400 years ago – and I wanted to be part of that history. It was an opportunity to have those mistakes or sins that had piled up since coming to Islam washed away; and it was an opportunity to come closer to God.

But before I could get closer to God, I had to negotiate with the Saudis.

The visa officials were very concerned that I wanted to visit Riyadh first, so I could travel with my mother-in-law, as part of a Saudi group undertaking *Hajj* in Mecca. They thought I might try to stay in the country illegally. I tried to convince them that I would be more than happy to leave Saudi Arabia the moment *Hajj* was over: I had my home. I was finally given the visas the day we travelled.

A time to die

We told our parents and employers about our prospective 'holiday' plans.

My mother was worried because she knew about *Hajj*: people died there. They died in a myriad of ways – dying in fires, dying in tunnels and dying in stampedes. She always watched the BBC News, which each year reported an up-to-date summary of the total deaths on the pilgrimage.

I explained to my employer that I couldn't be flexible about the timing for my annual leave as *Hajj* was fixed and happened just once a year. My boss already knew about *Hajj* too: she had an older Muslim friend, who kept going on *Hajj* in order to die. Disappointingly for this friend, each time she went, she remained steadfastly among the living. I understood why my boss's friend might be on a death mission. Given that we all have to die sometime, many consider *Hajj* to be an excellent place to pass away as Muslims believe we would then be leaving the world completely free of sins.[3]

But I was intending to return alive. Nevertheless, I had to make a will: it was part of the practical and spiritual preparation required to undertake *Hajj*. I duly made my will in England. Just five minutes before we walked out of the door of Julian's parents' home in Riyadh, to fly to Mecca, Julian remembered he needed to make a will too. He bequeathed all his worldly possessions in one sentence using a Post-It note. He left it in the house, and realized at the airport that he had omitted to get it witnessed.

Getting into a state

Our *Hajj* group comprised of approximately 250 Saudi women, the same number of Saudi men, and us: Julian, his mother, a British Pakistani couple, called Sadia and Harris, who were good friends of ours from England, and myself.

The trip was meant to be an intensely spiritual journey as well as a physical one. On the way to Jeddah, we passed the point at which all *Hajjis*, or pilgrims, had to be in a sacred state of consecration known as *ihram*. While in this state, we had to have the intention to perform *Hajj*, wear the appropriate clothes, repeat a particular Arabic prayer and observe several unusual restrictions.

We women could wear anything as long as it covered up our bodies. Julian's mother fitted in well: she wore a black *abaya* and black *hijab* for the occasion. She did stand out a little among the Saudis: she showed her face. Sadia wore a long white loose top over white and equally loose trousers: she stood out rather more, as all the Saudis were in black. Then there was me. No one had told me that women would be mainly in black or white and it didn't occur to me to ask. I just knew that women's dress on *Hajj* should be simple. So in Riyadh, I had spent five minutes at the shops, picking up three long-sleeved and full-length plain dresses of different colours: red, green and blue. People saw me coming from a long way off.

The men didn't have the perennial female problem of wondering what to wear. While in the state of *ihram*, they had to wear only two white pieces of cloth or towelling: one draped over the shoulder leaving the right shoulder exposed, the other wrapped around the waist. And that was it: no safety pins were allowed, nor even any underwear. It emphasized the absolute equality before God among pilgrims of different nationalities, colours and wealth backgrounds. On *Hajj*, even Saudi kings would be wearing just those two towels. At least it made it easy to pack the suitcase. It also made it virtually impossible to spot the man in your life in a crowd.

A few Saudis who had not boarded already clad in the white towels made sure they had popped into the aeroplane toilets to change.

Here we come

Throughout the aeroplane, the passengers started repeatedly reciting the *Hajj dua*,[4] the same supplication to God that Muhammad had made many years ago. Fortunately, I had been practising: it was short, rhythmic and not too hard for me to learn.

I joined in with the prayer. *'Labbayk Allahumma, Labbayk. Labbayka laa shareeka laka labbayk. Innal hamda wanni'mata laka wal mulk. La shareeka lak.'* I knew the English meaning by heart too: 'Here I am at Your service, O Lord. Here I am at Your service. There is no partner with you. Here I am at Your service. All Praise, Grace and Sovereignty belong to you. There is no partner with you.'

From all over the world, pilgrims were now converging on Mecca ready for the start of *Hajj*. We were coming to God to worship Him together. And we were all saying the same prayer in the same language. We were one global community.

Temporary abstinence

For the duration of *ihram*, I now had to practise self-restraint – and I was meant to take this new-found discipline away with me afterwards. There were a few things that I had to refrain from temporarily but completely.

Perfume was forbidden – even my normally perfumed shampoo and my much-loved moisturizer was out of bounds. Thank goodness for the English institution of Boots the chemist, where I had stocked up on fragrance-free soap, deodorant and moisturizer. I even found some fragrance-free toothpaste for the occasion. I also had to avoid killing animals for food (5:95), but that was not a problem: I was not being put in charge of the catering arrangements.

And I had to abstain from any sexual contact with my spouse – not even a touch (2:197). While sex between husbands and wives was usually considered a blessing in Islam, thoughts during *Hajj* were meant to remain steadfastly on more spiritual matters. Non-sexual touching was still acceptable – in fact it would be virtually essential once *Hajj* started, as we would want to be holding on to each other in among the crowds to ensure we never became separated.

The penance for a kiss or for wearing perfume was slaughtering a goat; the penance for sex was slaughtering a camel, in addition to having to repeat the *Hajj* again. It really didn't seem worth it. Julian and Harris had to make a special effort to postpone all thoughts and discussion about cars and computers: this was the time to concentrate on the soul. The two of them went through gadget-withdrawal symptoms together.

Learning to worship

I needed to occupy my time while we waited to pass through '*Hajj* Control' on arrival in Jeddah airport. It didn't seem the right kind of atmosphere to be reading a novel or even the newspaper. I decided to learn the 109th *surah* from the Qur'an in Arabic: it was one of the chapters that I had struggled with for ages.

Because I still couldn't read the original cursive Arabic script of the Qur'an, I was learning with an English version of the Arabic letters. Several younger Saudi girls noticed what I was doing and they summoned a couple of others to come and look at the sight. 'I didn't know that some people really read the Qur'an like this,' one said, laughing. 'At school, we sometimes write Arabic this way for a joke.' They smiled and I smiled back: I hoped they were laughing with me rather than at me.

I found the Arabic in that particular chapter difficult because the word *abud*, meaning 'worship', kept appearing, but in lots of different forms – the ending changed, like German, according to the sentence construction. The only way I could learn it was by thinking of it as an *abud* sandwich: the third and fifth lines were the same and they sandwiched two entirely different versions of the word *abud* in between. It was all very complicated.

The English meaning was much more straightforward. The verses were addressed to people in Mecca who worshipped idols at the time Muhammad was starting to talk about One God. The idol-worshippers wanted him to be like them; Muhammad didn't feel the same way.

> Say: O you who deny the truth!
> I do not worship that which you worship,
> and neither do you worship that which I worship!
> And I will not worship that which you have [ever] worshipped,
> and neither will you [ever] worship that which I worship.
> Unto you, your moral law, and unto me, mine !

(109:1–6)

Once I had finished learning this chapter in both Arabic and English, I felt I had achieved something significant. Muhammad had said that this particular chapter was equal in meaning to a quarter of the Qur'an.[5] Among others, I already knew another key chapter – the one

I had recited to the Syrian man in the coffee shop, which was equivalent to one-third of it. Mathematically, I was now over half-way.

Escalating the issue

On the bus journey between Jeddah and Mecca, we passed road signs saying: 'Non-Muslims turn off here.' I wouldn't like to be told I couldn't travel somewhere simply because I was Muslim – or because I wasn't. But it did mean that I was on my way to a place where every single person shared the same belief in God, and the same belief in His prophets. And we would all be praying to our Creator together.

Our entrance to Mecca was not an auspicious one: we ended up in a giant underground car park, and had to make our way out using an escalator. Thousands of people from different countries were milling around us; many had congregated at the foot of this escalator, blocking the ascent. The tour guide from a North African group explained the problem to me: these particular *Hajjis* had never seen an escalator – they had no idea how to get on it and no idea where it might be taking them. I tried my best to practise patience and understanding.

When we eventually emerged, we saw a sign on one wall: we were entering the Masjid al-Haram, 'the Sacred Mosque'. I was aware that *haram* had another, rather different, meaning: it meant forbidden. It made me think that I might need to get to grips with these worlds in their original language after all.

The uniting cube

Inside the Great Mosque was the Ka'bah. It was a large yet simple cube, covered in black cloth with decorated trimmings. Yet under the black cloth were thousands of years of history, tracing the prophets sent throughout time. As a Muslim, I believed the Ka'bah was originally built by Adam; it was rebuilt by Abraham and his son Ismail (2:127); and it was rebuilt again by the tribes of Mecca with Muhammad.

Thousands of Muslims were already in the mosque, all turned in prayer to form ever smaller concentric circles around the Ka'bah. It looked like they were praying to this cube, but I knew that the Ka'bah was simply a focal point, a way to unite the diverse Muslim community to pray to the One God. In England, I always tried to face the Ka'bah too: the concentric circles around the Ka'bah spread out around the world. God was everywhere – but we had to face somewhere. The Ka'bah united us, across both time and space.

Men and women were praying next to each other around the mosque, and particularly close to the Ka'bah. Sometimes, women ended up in front of the men. I had experienced several mosques in England, and found that frustratingly there often wasn't anywhere at all for women to pray – when there was space allocated to women, it was frequently a shabby room upstairs. Yet here, in Islam's holiest place, women were praying while standing right next to – or even in front of – the men. In England, the men would be saying *haram* – and they would be meaning 'forbidden' rather than 'sacred'.

I walked towards the Ka'bah, and found a small space where I could perform two optional *raka'ah* of prayer. As always, I was meant to keep my eyes down, staying focused on the ground directly in front of me, but now I couldn't stop my eyes being drawn inexorably towards the Ka'bah. I hoped God would understand; God was surely the Most Merciful.

Retracing the steps

Before *Hajj* officially started, we had time to perform *Umrah*, a much smaller version of *Hajj*, which could be completed in as little as two hours if there weren't hordes of people. But the hordes were there –

the place was packed, even though it was midnight when we began. Conventional ways and times to do things didn't seem to matter in Mecca: life was organized completely around prayer times and the rites of pilgrimage.

The first rite of *Umrah* was called *tawaf*: we had to walk around the Ka'bah seven times, in an anticlockwise direction, retracing the steps of Abraham and Muhammad taken thousands and hundreds of years ago respectively. We were careful not to get caught up in the ring of people circulating the Ka'bah for hours, carrying the old and the infirm on stretchers above their heads. I walked round and round, passing women who had their country of origin identified clearly on their *hijab*, so that they could find their tour group more easily in the crowds. As I walked alongside people from China, the Philippines, Indonesia, Pakistan, America, France and Nigeria, I could hear the sound of their prayers in Arabic alongside my own. I delighted in knowing the words of the prayers they were saying. I was used to being in environments where the common language was English: for the first time I found it was a different language that was uniting the people.

I then went to pray two *raka'ah* of ritual prayer near the Ka'bah, at the Station of Abraham where – as he had raised the foundations – he had prayed to God, asking for God's forgiveness and Mercy (2:127–8). I prayed how Muhammad had subsequently prayed at that very same spot over 1,400 years ago: I recited in Arabic exactly the same chapters of the Qur'an that he had. One of them was the one I had just learnt at the airport: 'Unto you, your moral law, and unto me, mine!' (109:6).

Satisfying a thirst

I then tasted the refreshing and distinctive Zam Zam water that had been coming from a nearby aquifer for the last 4,500 years. Its existence was still a miracle, in a land where there were no rivers. It hadn't occurred to me to bring a cup and so I drank out of the same mug that many of the three million pilgrims going on *Hajj* with me would have already used. I prayed that I wouldn't get ill.

I was now ready to complete the second rite, walking seven times between two hills known as Safa and Marwah. I was re-enacting the story of Abraham's wife Hajar. Upon God's instructions, Hajar had been left in the desert with their small son Ismail. Hajar ran frantically backwards and forwards between these same hills, looking out for any passing caravans and for water to quench her baby's thirst and calm his cries. A spring of water arose where the baby had been lying. In her efforts to staunch this flow of water, Hajar shouted 'Zam Zam': it meant 'Stop, Stop!' To this day, the water still runs.

As we left, there remained endless streams of people moving seamlessly and quietly around the Ka'bah, and making the rounds between Safa and Marwah.

Hajj: day one

We got back on our coach for a journey of just a few kilometres and arrived in Mina. The annual *Hajj*, the busiest time of year in Mecca and Mina, was about to begin.

I had expected to feel the *Hajj* atmosphere from the moment it started: I was among millions of people who had come from all over the world to perform the same rites. But I was cocooned in a building, with my group of Saudi women. It was clear I was going to have to search within myself to find the spiritual experience I was looking for.

On that first day, there were no specific *Hajj* rites to complete. I spent the day indoors – reading, learning and discussing. It was surprisingly tiring: I was not used to sitting in one place for a long period of time. Julian's mother was sitting next to me; she became immersed in a discussion with a Saudi lady about what constituted *hijab*. What about covering your hair while showing your face?

'*Haram,*' the lady declared. What about wearing the *niqab*, covering your mouth and showing only your eyes? '*Haram,*' she said, adamantly. And what about those Saudi women who covered their face with two layers of black cloth? '*Haram!*' came the even more vehement response. 'The correct way is to cover your face with one layer of black cloth,' explained my mother-in-law's debating partner. There didn't seem much scope for discussion.

I stepped outside briefly with the Saudi women in the afternoon to find the sky filled with smoke. We heard that at least 300 people camping in tents had died in a fire and a further 1,500 had been injured in the subsequent rush to escape. I presumed the BBC was meticulously recording the details. We lost power and running water for three hours as a result. Our group leader told us we needed some hardship to really feel *Hajj*: I knew our hardship was minimal.

Hajj: day two

The second day was the Day of Arafat, the most important day of the *Hajj*. '*Hajj* is Arafat,' Muhammad had said.[6]

We were going to stand on the very plain where Muhammad had given his last sermon,[7] while completing his final *Hajj*. His words had been spoken hundreds of years ago but the meaning of the words was for all time. In his speech he had emphasized the equality of all humanity:

> All of you belong to the line of Adam and Adam was created from dust. An Arab is not better than a non-Arab, nor is a white better than a black or a black better than a white, except by *Taqwa* (awareness of God and good actions).

And now here I was, praying alongside three million others, including the Arab, the non-Arab, the white and the black. The men were wearing their towels, most women were dressed in white, the Saudi women were in black – and I was in red. We were all equal before God.

Yet, in terms of material comfort, some of us were more equal than others. There were hundreds of thousands on the plain of Arafat, supplicating to God in the searing heat, but our group – along with countless others – were accommodated for the day in large private tents. The shade from the sun was great but the loss of community spirit was perhaps greater. Nevertheless, I stood up to make my own personal prayers to God for hours, praying for people that I knew – and those that I did not – to receive all that was good in this world and in the Hereafter.

I stopped, mentally exhausted, shortly before the time for the congregational prayer. I had to queue up at the single tap designated for our tent, in order to perform my *wudu*, the ritual washing before prayer. I was there for ages, but the queue didn't seem to be getting any shorter. I was learning the hard way that not all cultures were as expert at queuing as the English – my politeness wasn't getting me anywhere. Saudi women kept pushing in front of me. After 45 minutes, two women noticed what was happening and led me straight to the front. The other Saudis in the line stood aside to let me pass, smiling sympathetically at my inability to do it 'their' way. I finished just in time to join the communal prayer.

Pebble picking

And then at sunset we all left. All three million of us. We left for the plain of Muzdalifah. It was only 3 km away yet it took my group five hours to reach due to the incredible volume of both human and automotive traffic, all heading in the same direction at the same time.

There was nothing in Muzdalifah. It was still an open plain. There were no buildings, no tents, no coffee shops and no restaurants. There were public toilets, although it took an hour to reach the front of the queue – even for a Saudi. But apart from the toilets there were just pebbles.

I was in Muzdalifah primarily to pick up the pebbles: I would need

70 of them over the coming days. The selected pebbles were meant to be no larger than a pea – I started choosing carefully. And then one Saudi woman designated herself as my personal pebble consultant. She gestured that my first one was too small, and that my next similar-sized one was too big. This was very confusing. I decided to ignore these unsolicited comments and carry on collecting – taking a couple extra just in case I lost a few along the way. When I had finished, I lay down on a small space on the large rug brought by the tour group leader and, surrounded by three million others, attempted to rest.

Hajj: day 3

In the early hours of the morning, the tour bus took our group back to Mina.

The guide came by to collect some money. We needed to pay him for arranging the slaughter of a cow on our behalf. Abraham was so ready to submit to God's will that he had been prepared to sacrifice his own son. God then substituted a ram and Abraham killed the animal instead (37:102–111). Now it was our turn to make the animal sacrifice. The meat was going to be distributed to the poor.

I was still tired: sleep was scarce on *Hajj*. But I needed all my energy for the final ritual that had to be completed before I could get out of the state of *ihram*. I had to stone the first of three pillars, known collectively as the *Jamarat,* or Stone-heaps, which symbolized the Devil, Satan.

I was about to re-enact another key episode in the life of Abraham – Abraham had encountered Satan at the first Stone-heap in Mina. There were various stories about the occasion when they met:[8] perhaps Abraham met Satan after leaving Hajar and Ismail in the desert; perhaps Abraham was on his way to perform *Hajj*; or perhaps he met Satan when he was taking his son to be sacrificed. Regardless, three times Satan challenged Abraham as to the rationality of his actions; three times, Angel Gabriel said to Abraham 'Pelt him'; three times Abraham stoned Satan. Twice, Satan then disappeared and reappeared in a different place – hence the three *Jamarats* – the third time he did not reappear. Abraham continued undaunted.[9]

I knew the stoning had personal significance for each of us too. It symbolically represented our internal striving to remain believing in God and, despite all temptation to do otherwise, to keep on the 'straight path'.

The first *Jamarat* was crowded: tens of thousands of people had arrived there before us. The Indonesian women had worked out how to make the most effective progress: they linked arms and forged through the crowds. Julian, his mother and I followed immediately in their wake. Once we were close to the *Jamarat*, we found many people were winding themselves up into a state of rage against Satan before they threw their pebbles. One man was hurling his sandals instead, screaming at Satan for all the bad things Satan had made him do to his family: for him, Satan was a convenient excuse.

A new look

We emerged from the *Jamarat* unscathed and then needed to look for a barber for Julian. It was not difficult to find one: there were hundreds of them, lined up on the road leading from the *Jamarat*. The barbers knew that all the men performing *Hajj* were going to want a hair cut after the first stoning: the restrictions of *ihram* would then be immediately lifted. Most men asked for their heads to be completely shaved; Julian opted for a modest trim. He couldn't imagine going back to the office in London sporting a 'skinhead' look. Julian went to back to his accommodation to change out of his white towels, shower and don a cool white Arab *thobe*.

I needed to have a hair cut too. I went back to my building to see if someone could do it there. Inside, women were busy cutting huge amounts of each other's hair in an atmosphere of happy chaos. I asked my mother-in-law to help; she obligingly cut off a couple of locks for me. I could now get out of *ihram* – and I went off to wash my hair with perfumed shampoo.

Letting our hair down

This third day of the *Hajj* rituals was the day of *Eid ul Adha*, the Festival of the Sacrifice.

I thought I knew about this annual *Eid*: I celebrated it in England. I had always thought that this festival marked the culmination of *Hajj*, yet now *Eid* had arrived and I was still in the middle of the pilgrimage. It dawned on me that that *Eid ul Adha* was actually marking the completion of the day of Arafat. And it was commemorating Abraham's willingness to sacrifice his son, despite the temptations that came his way; it was celebrating Abraham's total submission to God.

All the pilgrims were out of *ihram*: we could finally enjoy ourselves. But, unlike in England, we didn't have a party, we didn't have a get together and we didn't even have any special food. However, the group leader did hand out *Eid* presents to all of the women: we received a pair of black gloves and a pair of black 'Fashion' knee-high tights. I packed my gifts to take home as souvenirs.

In the evening I started to get to know those of my Saudi room-mates who were brave enough to try out their limited English language skills on me. One explained how most of the women in the group juggled their studies or work with marriage and children. Another woman in her twenties explained the variety of career opportunities that were available to them: 'Teaching, teaching or nursing – we don't have much choice,' they said, sadly. I appreciated the freedom I had in England to choose my own career.

Hajj: day 4

The day after *Eid*, I had to visit all three *Jamarats*, throwing a total of 21 pebbles in the process. The expedition was remarkably calm and uneventful: no one near me was hit by flying sandals; no one was overwrought.

And then it was time to visit Mecca, to make another *tawaf*, walking around the Ka'bah seven times. When we had visited the Grand Mosque a few days earlier, the *Hajj* had not yet begun, and I had noticed many *Hajj* pilgrims sleeping in the mosque. *Hajj* was only obligatory for those who could afford it: perhaps all the pilgrims' money had been spent on travelling to Mecca. But once *Hajj* started, I knew that every *Hajji* had to spend each night – except the pebble-collecting night – in Mina. The mosque in Mecca was now a lot less crowded; the homeless Muslims had had to move elsewhere.

As I performed *tawaf,* I said the Muslim creed over and over again in Arabic. It just rolled off the tongue: *'La ilaha illa Allah.'* 'There is no God but God.' It was identical in both meaning and construction to the first of the Ten Commandments with which I had been brought up from childhood: 'You shall have no other God but Me.' At the most basic and also most important level, the believers in one God were united.

Afterwards, I went to pray again at the Station of Abraham and then repeated the same route between Safa and Marwah that Abraham's wife Hajar had chosen. The whole area was heaving with people: I couldn't rush. Along with the millions of other pilgrims, I slowly journeyed back to Mina to spend the night.

Hajj: day 5

On the penultimate day of *Hajj*, I only had to throw 21 pebbles. I anticipated a relatively relaxing day. I was wrong.

There was chaos at the first *Jamarat*. Pilgrims had waited to throw their pebbles until midday. Many were then aiming to complete the rituals before the next congregational prayer began, which was due to take place just a few hours later, so they could travel to Mecca immediately afterwards. People were arriving with heavy suitcases and sun umbrellas, which were pointing dangerously close to people's eyes. A small infant was crying from the scorching heat. Julian, his mother, our British friends and I surged forwards with the crowd, almost all of us losing our sandals in the process. We tried to breathe; we turned our faces upwards to catch some air.

One man passed by trying to go against the crowd. He was carrying a shoulder bag by a strap, which had now become wrapped around his neck; it was slowly strangling him. Sadia translated his heartfelt appeal made in Urdu. 'O Lord, I am going to die,' he cried out. 'My Lord, I am going to die.' There was nothing we could do: the sheer weight of the crowds was too strong for us to move even an arm. A woman in a wheelchair was pushed into the area and we were forced into an even smaller space to accommodate her. Now there was no longer space to turn our face towards the sky: for a minute, I thought I might die too. We finally threw seven of our pebbles and left the dense crowd with relief.

I had only completed one *Jamarat* stoning; there were still two more to go. Julian and Harris volunteered to do the others on behalf of the three women in our little group – and we gratefully accepted their offer. That afternoon, we heard that 30 people had died during the *Jamarat* stoning that day. The BBC did not record it.

Hajj: day 6

Many pilgrims had left Mina the day before to go to Mecca. Along with a million others, we waited until midday and then completed a fourth and final throwing of the stones at the *Jamarats*, without any dramatic incidents.

Then it was our turn to leave Mina. While we were still inside the building, I said my goodbyes to the Saudi women: I knew I would have no chance of recognizing them once we stepped outside due to their total body and face covering. Most of them even wore identical shoes. We made our final 'farewell' *tawaf* in Mecca before heading back to England.

On the plane home, I prayed to God: 'O God, please accept my *Hajj.*' I had tried my best to fulfil the rites exactly the way they had been performed by both Abraham and Muhammad but I was only human and may have made a mistake. I prayed for God's Mercy.

Sick but alive

I had one outstanding issue: before I had undertaken the *Hajj*, a Muslim woman had told me that if a pilgrim didn't get ill their *Hajj* wouldn't be accepted. Now I had completed *Hajj* yet I still felt completely healthy. I need not have been concerned: even though this comment was simply an 'old wives' tale', Julian and I became ill all too soon.

Immediately upon our return to England, we both suffered from a violent strain of 'flu, experiencing vivid hallucinations alongside a persistent and high fever. Like many Londoners, we didn't know many people in our local community, except our neighbours in the flats above us, who were out at work. I reverted to doing what I have done ever since I was a child – I asked for help from my mother. My mother changed her plans for two days and drove down to look after us: the first thing she did was to put the kettle on and make us a cup of tea. I think she was relieved we had come back alive.

Reports back home

When I recovered, I checked how the events of this year's *Hajj* had been reported in the British newspapers. The tent fire was the main story: there were photographs and articles about the deaths and destruction. *Eid* was mentioned briefly – one newspaper showed a large and graphic image of people slaughtering cows in a patch of dirt in Calcutta, with a caption underneath. It explained: 'Muslims across the world slaughter animals for *Eid ul Adha*.'

I was one of around 25,000 British citizens[10] who had been on the annual *Hajj* and one of over a billion people world-wide who had commemorated the sacrifice of Abraham – yet it was marked in the British press through reports of a fire and a dead Indian cow.

But I wasn't complaining: I was very happy I had completed the *Hajj* and made it back to England. And I had managed to fulfil this fifth pillar of Islam together with my husband, just before our little family began to expand.

6 Babes in Arms

'Verily, We have created [every one of] you out of dust, then out of a drop of sperm, then out of a germ-cell, then out of an embryonic lump complete [in itself] and yet incomplete so that We might make [your origin] clear unto you. And whatever We will [to be born] We cause to rest in the [mothers'] wombs for a term set [by Us], and then We bring you forth as infants and [allow you to live] so that [some of] you might attain to maturity.'

(Qur'an 22:5)

'A man came to the Prophet and asked: "Who among people is most entitled to kind treatment from me?" He answered: "Your mother." The man asked: "Then who?" He said: "Your mother." "Then who?" The man insisted. The Prophet replied: "Your mother." The man asked, "Then who?" The Prophet said, "Then your father."'[1]

(Saying of Muhammad)

Within eight months of completing the *Hajj* I became pregnant.

As soon as I found the result of my home pregnancy test was positive I performed two voluntary *raka'ah* of prayer to thank God for this special event – but I had to do this in the hallway as the flat was temporarily full with people staying over in every room. And then I booked an appointment to see the doctor, assuming she would need to verify it. The doctor told me that if my own test was positive she had no need to do another one. Her expression remained blank, and she then asked me her only question: 'Do you want your baby?' I was taken aback. 'Yes, I really want this baby, I'm very happy,' I replied. She finally relaxed and smiled. 'It's just that a third of all pregnancies in England are unwanted – I had to ask if you wanted yours. Congratulations.'

We wanted a bigger place to live to accommodate our prospective baby. We soon discovered we could only afford that if we moved out to the suburbs. And so we moved to a commuter town 30 minutes away from London, to a place called Woking. A new phase in my life – and my husband's life – was about to begin.

What's in a name?

One of our first responsibilities as prospective parents was to think of a name for our unborn baby.

Unlike some converts to Islam I had never changed my first name. I knew that as long as my name had an inoffensive and preferably positive meaning, it was fine to keep it. Muhammad had insisted on changing the name of a man previously known as Abdu Shams, but that name had the meaning 'Slave of the Sun' so it wasn't exactly Islamic.[2] Lucy meant 'light'. I knew other Muslim girls called 'Nur', which was Arabic for 'light': I figured that my name was no more or less 'Muslim' than theirs. I had therefore successfully resisted the exhortations of several Muslim taxi drivers to change my name.

But naming my own child was different: there was the Muslim community to consider and Julian and I wanted this baby eventually to feel part of it. We thought an Arabic first name and an English middle name would go a little way towards cementing the child's multifaceted identity. And so we started thinking about Arabic names.

'You are not going to call it Saddam, are you?' asked my mother, more than a little concerned about this process. I had never come across a British Muslim baby called Saddam: I looked up the name. Rather appropriately, it meant 'powerful ruler' or 'crusher' – not reflecting any of the positive qualities we were hoping for in our baby. But the name stuck: it became a family joke. Throughout the pregnancy, my parents would telephone and ask: 'And how is Saddam?' I would tell them that Saddam was doing well. Thank God, Saddam always was.

Planning ahead

My bump was expanding; I was due to go on maternity leave very soon. I was getting a drink from the office tea machine when my colleague Liz approached me. 'Can I ask you something?' Liz asked. 'Go on then.' I said, dubiously – it sounded like it was going to be personal. 'So you're Muslim, right?' I agreed I was: so far, so good. 'Can I ask you how you are going to bring up your child? Will he or she have to be Muslim too?'

I tried to think about it on the spot: I had no idea how I was going to bring up this child. At the antenatal classes I was learning about pain relief and how to give the imminent baby both milk and a bath. I had started to be concerned about what I would feed my baby once it started on 'proper' food as I barely knew how to cook. And I was already wondering how I would protect my child from drugs in schools. But – apart from considering different names – I hadn't even thought about the 'Muslim' issue. Now I did.

'Well, I'll have to bring this child up as a Muslim.' I told her. 'I do believe in Islam – and I would want my child to grow up believing in it too.' Liz frowned. 'But if your child didn't want to be Muslim, would that be OK?' 'Of course it would,' I replied, trying to sound like I wouldn't mind. 'Every child chooses their own path when they get older. But I'm hoping that this baby might eventually find that Islam makes some sense.' Liz laughed: she seemed relieved. We drank our tea together.

Labouring over Saddam

Once it was obvious I was going into labour Julian immediately got to work installing a dimmer switch that would operate the light in the baby's nursery – he thought our newborn would need it. Unfortunately he managed to fuse all the lights in the house in the process. After six hours of labouring in complete darkness, I left with Julian to go the hospital.

In the delivery room, I changed into my nightwear. I wanted to preserve some semblance of modesty even in labour, so I asked the midwife if I could keep my underwear on. She just chuckled: I was clearly a first-time mother.

As the labour progressed with complications I shut my eyes and tried not to think about the numerous different men who were appearing in the room to examine and discuss my nether regions. Islamically, though, I knew it was acceptable. While female doctors, consultants and anaesthetists would have been preferable, that principle of 'competing priorities' applied again: my health and the health of my baby were much higher priorities than covering up in front of the opposite sex.

Saddam never came along. The baby was a little girl and we gave her an Arabic first name, Safiyya, named after a Jewish wife of Muhammad. The name meant 'sincere friend'. Her middle name was Imogen, meaning 'innocent', named after a kind Christian friend of Julian's at university. The names – and their origins – seemed appropriate: we hoped that she would grow up to be a good friend to others; we also believed that Safiyya, like all children, had been born pure and innocent. However, our daughter was not born serene: her cries were deafening.

First time grannies

My friend Lena, another English convert to Islam, gave birth to her son in the same week that Safiyya was born. She named her half-

English, half-Sudanese baby Ibrahim – Arabic for Abraham, a central figure in Judaism, Christianity and Islam.

Lena's mother was delighted to become a grandmother but not completely happy: she had hoped for an English-looking grandchild with a rather more English-sounding name. Lena told me her mother was calling him Ibbotson: writing the name in his New Baby card, writing it on the back of a framed picture she gave to him, and calling him Ibbotson to his face. Lena was concerned and she knew that once Ibrahim grew up a little he would be correcting Granny himself. But fortunately, the issue was resolved: Lena started to refer to her son as Ibby and Granny was happy with that. Ibbotson disappeared for ever.

My friend Wendy – whom I had met while trying to learn Arabic in the Central Mosque in London over three years before – gave birth to her first child just two days after I had become a mother. She named her little girl Maryam, Arabic for Mary, the mother of Jesus. Her parents were determined to enjoy every moment of their new identity as grandparents – whatever their baby was called. And Wendy and I spent hours on the telephone, discussing the minutiae of our new life: feeding, crying, washing, nappies and sleeping – or, more accurately, our lack of it.

Julian and I held a party for our immediate families to celebrate the birth of Safiyya. Now I knew why I had been keeping the top layer of our wedding cake for the last five years. We thanked God for our healthy baby girl and tucked in.

Losing the baby weight

I was disappointed: it looked like I was still pregnant. My bump was very much there even though Safiyya was now in the outside world. I regretted that for most of my nine months of pregnancy, I had been eating more than enough for two.

I went to the local gym, determined to lose the extra kilos, wearing a loose long-sleeved top, tracksuit bottoms and a light scarf. When I went in the morning, I felt comfortable: the sessions were filled with women and retired older men; the TV station was tuned into daytime chat shows. But it was different in the evening: the large television screen was now filled with young girls writhing about with very little on – particularly during MTV's 'Sexy Young Things' Month', which seemed to be most of the time. I averted my eyes. And I had to avert my eyes in the women's changing room too: for Muslims, even among people of the same sex, those 'private parts' were strictly private.

Liquid lunch

With women, I only had to cover between the navel and the knee. I breastfed my baby everywhere and enjoyed the closeness. If I was out in public, Safiyya snuggled up inside my top; any exposed skin was covered with my scarf. Julian also used the ends of my scarf to clean his glasses – fortunately not at the same time.

Jeffery told me I shouldn't be feeding my baby in front of him: he said it was not Islamic. But he had only just married his Chinese fiancée Li-Jia two months before: he hadn't had to cope with babies. I carried on. Once Li-Jia started having children, she confidently and modestly breastfed in public too. Our babies were hungry and they needed feeding wherever they happened to be.

I joined the local branch of the National Childbirth Trust, known as the NCT, to meet up with other new mothers for mutual support and friendship. I discovered some women had perfect babies who slept for hours and ate infrequently – but I tried my best to avoid them. The rest of us worked through the myriad of baby sleeping and feeding problems; we discussed the dilemmas of returning to work; and we drank lots of cups of tea.

When our babies hit six months old, I noticed it was becoming less 'normal' to breastfeed. Safiyya breastfed less too – I had worked out how to make her baby food – but she still had the occasional feed. Once Safiyya was an active one-year-old even my own mother and sister became uncomfortable being around us if she was feeding. Breastfeeding became a clandestine activity, restricted to early mornings and child bedtimes – unless I happened to be with people who either didn't mind or who were doing it too. I knew lots of Muslims who fed their babies for a full two years, even if it was just once or twice a day. It was in line with advice from the World Health Organization[3] and it was also recommended in the Qur'an (2:233).

Attempting Arabic – again

I now had a renewed impetus to learn Arabic. I didn't want Safiyya to struggle with reading the Qur'an in its original language the way I had. And I imagined the blissful 'quality time' that she and I might eventually enjoy once we could read it together.

I found a weekly class taught by an educated Syrian lady, Mu'mina, referred to as 'Sister Mu'mina' as a mark of respect. She lived nearby, and her three children were at local schools. All her children had been given Arabic names – her teenage son's name meant 'like a lion'; he was called Osama. We brought our babies and toddlers to the lesson – they happily played around our feet, crawled over us and hit each other. In the meantime, Sister Mu'mina read a line of Qur'an, and her students repeated it as a group, word by word, before taking individual turns.

I dreaded my turn. All the 'born Muslim' women were able to read the words while I was still struggling with the alphabet. It took 10 minutes for me to say my single line. The teacher kept telling me 'Learn your letters'. I was going to have to do some homework. So during Safiyya's afternoon nap at home, I turned on the computer and followed a programme called *Al Qari, The Teacher*. I learnt not only my letters but also how to join them up. I had now reached the level of a six-year-old. And then I began to make real progress.

The original Arabic Qur'an came to life. I could read it myself; I could follow it when I heard other people recite. When I visited the British Museum, I was even able to read extracts from an ancient copy on display there – that book matched my copy exactly, letter for letter. I didn't have a perfect accent, but I could finally read the Qur'an – and I knew enough to help my own child one day do the same.

Mutually satisfying

After Sister Mu'mina had been through the translation and interpretation of the verses we had just read, she led us in a discussion about any topic that came up. The discussion almost always involved relationships and sex.

We were taught that according to Islam we didn't have to clean the house and we didn't have to cook: someone had to; it just didn't have to be us. And it was recommended that we rest in the early afternoon so we had lots of energy later for our children – and our husbands.

Our main duty was to satisfy our husbands in the bedroom. We must beautify ourselves for our husbands; we must never ever say no if they wanted 'intimate relations'. This advice felt like it had been lifted out of the English 1950s guides to being a good wife but I could see that it would contribute towards a happy home and marriage. Julian was quick to agree. One woman asked: 'And what about our husband's obligations to us?' Sister Mu'mina explained that those particular responsibilities were mutual, although the husband was exempt if he was physically exhausted or if he was then prevented from earning a living.[4] It all sounded very tiring; it made me want my afternoon nap.

Our teacher went on to say that if we believed in God and led good lives, we could choose to be next to our husbands in Paradise. And if we had been married to more than one husband during our lifetime, we could even choose which one to be next to.[5]

But we asked her: 'Will the men be choosing to be with their wives?' The national and international media[6] were repeatedly telling us how certain men would be getting seventy-two virgins in Paradise. It became clear that the Qur'an never mentioned the number of virgins anywhere, although it did say there would be dark-eyed *houris* around in Paradise (55:72–4; 56:22). I took out my own translation of the Qur'an by Muhammad Asad, the Austrian scholar. Asad's detailed research had led him to translate the word *houris* as 'pure companions'; he explained that the word had both feminine and masculine roots. The *houris* would be pure, they would be male and female and they would be companions in Paradise for us all.

From the multitude of descriptions of Paradise in the Qur'an involving gardens, flowing rivers and shade, we could quickly get the idea that Paradise was going to be an unimaginably happy place for anyone who made it there. The main point was that none of us knew who would be there anyway: we should therefore all be focusing on leading good lives right here and right now. We were suitably chastened.

Differences that divide

The class was sociable and I came to know many of the women. Two other English converts with equally English names began to attend the lesson: Claire, from the town next to Woking and Rachel from a small village in the countryside nearby.

In the class, I met my first ever Shia Muslim, Layla, who was a student attending university nearby. Muslims in England had often asked me if I was Shia, once they found out that my husband had some – albeit tenuous – links with Shia-dominated Iran and they had usually looked relieved when I said I wasn't. I called myself a Sunni but never particularly want to be identified as either: I was just a Muslim.

I invited Layla to my house for tea and during our conversation I asked her what the Shia were all about. Who were they? And why were they different to the majority; the Sunnis? Layla had no idea; she told me she was Shia simply because her parents were. We found out the answers.

Around one in 10 of the world's Muslims were Shia, all sharing the same core beliefs as the rest of the Muslims who were Sunni: all Muslims believed in God, believed that Muhammad is the final Prophet, and observed the 'five pillars' of Islam.

But there were differences between Shia and Sunni Muslims, which were originally historical and political.[7] After the death of Muhammad, the majority of Muslims accepted that his trusted companion Abu Bakr was the first Caliph, leader of the Muslims. But the Shias thought Muhammad's cousin and son-in-law Ali should have been the first one and that all subsequent Caliphs should have been Ali's descendants. The differences continued over time: in the battle of Karbala, 50 years after Muhammad had died, Ali's son Hussein was killed by the cousin of Uthman, the third Caliph, who had been recognized by Sunnis alone as legitimate.

Today, the division between the Shias and Sunnis had become more than historical: there were differences in both the belief and the practice of Islam. One difference was the Shia belief in an *imamate*, a formal hierarchy of clergy who were considered inerrant interpreters of law and tradition – the Sunnis didn't have any clergy, let alone an infallible one. Another was the Shia emphasis on martyrdom and suffering, focusing on the violent deaths of Ali and his son Hussein. Shia Muslims also have a slightly different call to prayer, a slightly different way to complete the ritual washing before prayer and a slightly different method of performing the ritual prayer itself. Shias were comfortable combining the prayers, often praying three times a day rather than five.

Layla and I could see the distinct differences but we could also see that both Shia and Sunni were Muslims. We were part of one community; we believed in one God and all His Prophets. We carried on attending Qur'an class together.

Organized chaos

I went back to work three days a week, planning my work schedule around the weekly activities that I went to with Safiyya. We still attended the Qur'an class; I also took her to the local church playgroup, Bethany Babes. We rarely missed our 45 minutes on Wednesdays at Tumble Tots, an energetic soft-play session – Safiyya climbed and jumped and rolled head-first into tunnels. Once a week, I met up with other Muslim women at an informal 'mother-and-toddler' group. And I caught up with other friends and neighbours over lunch or tea. I arrived back at work exhausted after my two days off. None of my colleagues were sympathetic.

Bethany Babes, the church playgroup, was highly organized, supportive and friendly. The preschoolers sang a prayer to God before they tucked into their juice and biscuits; the adults then enjoyed tea and a chat while the children played. Safiyya loved it. I loved it too, except when my turn on the craft rota came around: I had to spend a stressful evening preparing for the toddlers to make something that would bear even a slight resemblance to a caterpillar, a boat or a tree.

My sister Julie came by with her two young children every couple of months – people always commented on how different we looked. We did look different: she was tall and dark-haired; I was short and wore a scarf. On three occasions, I brought along my English Muslim friends Lena, Wendy and Claire, all of whom happened to wear a scarf; three times, other mothers asked me: 'Is this your sister?'

The world turns upside-down

The Tumble Tots organizer was aware I was Muslim. While Safiyya was hanging upside-down off a ladder, I mentioned to her that I would like to bring my mother along to Tumble Tots soon. Before agreeing, she asked me: 'Does your mother speak English?' I replied with a straight face: 'Yes, my mother's English is pretty good.' As soon as I answered, she realized what she had said: we both laughed.

And then, the day before the next session, everything changed. It was a Tuesday. It was September 11, 2001.

I watched the planes crashing repeatedly into the World Trade Center; I watched the continuous television reports about burning buildings, heroic firemen, dead and injured workers. Information was still trickling in when I went to my regular afternoon Muslim mother-and-toddler group: we talked about what we knew, and those we knew who might be affected – and we all hoped that Muslims had had nothing to do with it. I came back home to find that the media was now reporting it was a terrorist attack. A Muslim terrorist attack. It was a tragedy on a huge scale. I wanted to speak to my mother to empathize together with those living, working and dying in New York. But I didn't call. I thought she might feel that since I was Muslim, I was in some way associated with this terrible act of destruction.

That evening, my mother telephoned me. 'Are you OK, Lucy?' she asked. 'I've been so worried about you.' Her motherly concern for my welfare amidst this global trauma brought tears to my eyes.

The next day I went back to Tumble Tots, with a heavy heart. The leader had a suggestion for me: 'Why don't the Arabs get their own airline? At least then if they wanted to kill people, they would only be blowing up themselves.' In response, I mentioned with a smile that Arabs did own several airlines already – and that non-Arabs often travelled on them too.

I then missed two Tumble Tots sessions in a row. The organizer was so relieved to see me when I came back. 'I thought I had offended you,' she said. 'I explained to other mums what I said to you; they told me off and I've been feeling terrible.' I told her why I had been away: the first Wednesday, Safiyya had been ill; then the following week she had decided to swallow a clock battery and I had to take her to have an emergency X-ray in hospital, although I couldn't stand near Safiyya while she was being X-rayed as, once again, I was pregnant.

Birth by the bath

Five months later, my son Asim was born – at home. Two English community midwives came to help although one stayed in our sitting room for most of the time, ready to act in case of an emergency. The other midwife was warm and unobtrusive, only stepping in when her assistance became essential. During labour, my husband followed me around with a sheet of tarpaulin in case of damage to our carpets. Apart from that distraction, the entire home birthing process was relaxed and – importantly for me – natural, uncomplicated and private.

When the contractions intensified, I repeatedly recited the first half of the Muslim creed to help me to stay calm: '*La ilaha illa Allah*' – there is no God but God. And I made supplications to God for my baby and those around me. The contractions still hurt, but at least my mind was occupied.

Julian knew he would have his own responsibilities immediately after the birth. 'Which ear do I do it in?' he asked, as I was in the final throes of labour. 'I've forgotten.' Julian was talking about the practice of reciting the *adhan*,[8] the Muslim call to prayer, in the new baby's right ear, so that the first words our baby heard in life would be the declaration of faith in God. I threw him a book, which I knew would have the answers – I was a little too preoccupied to look myself. Asim appeared on the laminated floor of our bathroom: our carpets were untouched.

Julian knew what he had to do next – he rubbed a juicy date against Asim's lips.[9] Muhammad did this himself for newborns:[10] the sugar content helped to soothe feelings of pain; and it meant that the first thing a baby tasted in life was the sweetness of nature. Once the midwife had checked that Julian wasn't intending to feed Asim the whole date, she relaxed and watched the scene with interest.

Out with the knife

On the seventh day, Julian shaved Asim's head: the Islamic tradition was to donate the equivalent weight of the baby's hair in silver or gold to charity. We made a rough estimate of the weight and value, and made a donation.[11] The skinhead look did make Asim seem quite scary. Fortunately, it was winter time: Asim could legitimately spend the next month wearing a woolly hat.

As Muslims, we also wanted to follow Muhammad's recommendation to slaughter a sheep,[12] as a way of thanking God for the birth. When Safiyya was born, Julian had spoken to the nearby *halal* butcher: the butcher had organized the slaughter, and had then asked another member of the community to cook the meat. It fed everyone who came to our local mosque for one day. But now we thought it might be better if all the meat could go to people who were really in need. Islamically, we could choose what we did with the food, as long as we gave at least some of it to others. My in-laws had recently moved from Saudi Arabia to Iran: in that country, there were thousands who were hungry. And so Julian asked his mother to order two sheep in Iran and arrange for the meat to be distributed to the needy. She did and we were thankful: to God, to my in-laws and to the butcher.

The final ritual associated with the birth of our baby boy was circumcision.[13] It was a custom of Muhammad – and of Jesus – that the *hadiths* encouraged us to complete as soon as possible after the birth. And so we did.

The local hospital ran a weekly private circumcision clinic, opening an hour earlier for that day to complete the operations before the rest of the hospital opened. I booked Asim for an appointment when he was exactly two weeks old. The doctor assured me it would be fine: 'It hurts the mother more than the child,' he told me. I wasn't so sure. He carried Asim to his room, leaving Julian and myself waiting outside. Asim emerged a few minutes later, whimpering.

For the next two hours, Asim was very unhappy. My mother had arrived the night before so that she could look after Safiyya while we were at the hospital. Now Asim was home, she took him upstairs to change his nappy. She was surprised when she took his hat off: 'I could have sworn that he had been born with a bit more hair,' she said. And then my mother found blood in his nappy. I felt terrible: it was bad enough to see my little boy in pain, but I thought my mother would view Islam as truly barbaric to hurt a baby. I knew that circumcision used to be a British tradition, particularly among upper and middle-class families, but traditions change. Fortunately, by lunchtime, Asim was fine.

Giving and taking life

When Asim was nine months old, in October 2002, I found out I was pregnant again.

An hour before I did the test, my parents had rung. They told me that a family friend of ours, whose wedding my parents had attended only five weeks earlier, had just lost her husband. Ian had been killed in a nightclub, in the Bali bombings. Our friend Polly was alive but was suffering from severe burns covering almost half of her body: she had been airlifted to Australia to begin weeks of specialist treatment. It was shocking news and even more shocking to me that these senseless injuries and deaths seemed to be entirely due to the actions of Muslims.

And then, just two minutes after I examined the test result, I received a telephone call from one of my local Muslim friends, Allia. Allia had been five months pregnant: the doctor had now told her that her little baby had died while still in the womb. I was so sad to hear of her loss.

The closeness of all these events literally took away all my strength. God creates life and he takes away life in an instant. Now I was pregnant with another innocent life – what kind of world was I bringing this new baby into? I could no longer stand. I lay on the floor and prayed that some good would come out of it all.

Health check

Eight months later, my third child Amaani was born. She was born at home, in exactly the same spot on the bathroom floor as Asim. Julian still had to remind himself at the last minute about what he was meant to say in which ear.

As Amaani and I recovered in the bedroom a midwife asked for permission to give Amaani the BCG vaccination. I found that strange: my other children hadn't been given it. So the midwife handed me a pamphlet on the subject. It explained the vaccination is given to babies 'who are more likely than the general population to come into contact with TB.' I asked her: 'Why is my baby any more likely to have this contact than anyone else?' My baby was British, with two British parents and four British grandparents; we lived in a suburban town. Surely it wasn't because Amaani was Muslim? She looked a bit embarrassed – she didn't give Amaani the injection.

For Amaani's two-month old routine check, I took her to see a neonatal doctor. 'Do you think your baby might be deprived of vitamin D?' the doctor immediately asked, when she saw us. 'You do have to be careful – deficiency occurs if there is insufficient exposure to sunlight.' I looked at Amaani: it was summer time, and I had dressed her in a pink cotton romper suit, which stopped just above the elbows and knees. I was in my jeans, long-sleeved top and a headscarf. I suggested to the doctor that she might have been thinking about the Muslim ladies who wore all black; I also explained that even though those women choose to cover themselves fully, their young children could wear anything. 'Of course,' she said, 'I'm sorry, I don't know too much about Islam. But I do know that Muslims don't drink alcohol – that sounds like an excellent idea.' As the doctor made a note of Amaani's key statistics, she went on to tell me a few of the alcoholic problems that had come her way. The next mother and baby waited outside.

Within the month, I was back at the doctor's surgery again. The regular doctors that I was used to were busy; I had to see a locum. As I struggled to get through the door, carrying one child and cajoling two, a male doctor in his fifties greeted me with the words: 'There was an old woman who lived in a shoe.' I knew the next line: it didn't look like he was paying me a compliment. He asked about my religion. But I wanted to know why Asim was developing a rash. I only had a five-minute appointment: in that time he prescribed Asim some cream while I gave him a potted version of the core Islamic beliefs. It was a relief to leave his office: the older two children were climbing all over me and Amaani needed feeding yet again.

Scene of the crime

When Amaani was three months old, two policemen in full uniform came to the door. They asked me if my husband lived at that address.

My mother was spending the day with me. Both of us thought something terrible had happened to Julian. My mother assumed he had had a serious accident; I thought he had been arrested. After the events of September 11, Lotfi Raissi, a Muslim who had been living near Heathrow, had been arrested by British police upon FBI instructions and spent months in Belmarsh Prison. Just before Amaani was born, the media had reported that Lotfi had been released from all charges.[14] Julian was innocent – but then, so was Lotfi. I was a little paranoid.

I was wrong and so was my mother. The police told me that they had caught two young men, aged 15 and 16, driving Julian's 50cc moped in the emergency lane of the M25 motorway. The moped was now impounded – and broken.

Julian came back from work early, and got a taxi to the police depot to retrieve his motorbike. After paying a fee of £150 to get the moped released, both Julian and the moped were given a lift back home by a van driver from the depot. With amusement, he recounted to me what the driver then told him on the way. 'They wouldn't be so quick to take other people's property again if we chopped a hand off each of them. We are way too soft.'

Unlike the van-driver, Julian and I were only qualified supporters of hand chopping as a deterrent to crime. There were so many criteria that had to be met first: at the very least, the punishment had to be implemented with justice, in a Muslim country, where people were not stealing as a result of poverty. A European scholar, Tariq Ramadan, was calling for a moratorium on all *Sharia*-specified punishments:[15] he felt that not only had the exact conditions and contexts not been agreed but also that the punishments were usually implemented with impunity only against women and the poor.

But the court was indeed soft: while the youngest teenager was released without charge, the other lad was made to pay one pound a week towards Julian's costs. The money never materialized – perhaps he was too poor.

The English au pair

After my third maternity leave I wanted to work for my previous company on a consultancy basis; I also started a flexible teacher-training course. I decided I needed some help – I needed an au pair. I spent hours trawling the Internet-based au pair agencies, which matched prospective au pairs with prospective families. I focused on the qualities I was looking for: someone with caring and compassion, who took her responsibilities seriously, who was honest, and who had stacks of energy. Through a website, I found Michelle and Michelle found me.

Unusually for an au pair in England, Michelle was English. Michelle was respectful of our Muslim customs. She always covered up her legs, Julian never saw her in her nightwear and she was happy not to bring alcohol or pork in to the house. She was attempting to give up smoking but, in the meantime, agreed to smoke outside the house. Michelle threw herself into her work: loving the children, taking them to the park and dancing with them. She got to know many of their little friends and was happy to look after them sometimes too. And she helped me with the recurring piles of washing-up. It was all going well.

Finding God

Michelle began to use her free time to develop her faith in Christianity. My neighbour Susie, who was always ready to help anybody where she could, kindly offered to take her to church and so they went together. Michelle and I now had to coordinate our social lives, taking into account the times of her church services. She even talked about fasting in Advent. Safiyya was affected by Michelle's enthusiasm and attempted to read the Bible: she started writing out a few words from Genesis on her toy blackboard. I hadn't expected any of this.

And then one day Michelle told me she wanted to become Muslim. I hadn't expected that either.

Michelle explained that she hadn't managed to convince herself completely about Christianity – she couldn't understand why Jesus had died for her or why her church was asking the congregation to pray for Muslims to be saved. Her interest in Islam wasn't entirely new: she had deliberately considered joining three different families, all of whom were Muslim, before ending up with us. She already knew a little about Islam and had discovered more while staying in our house. Michelle told me she had been asking Safiyya questions and had picked up from the bookshelf a few of our 'beginner's books' on Islam.

I was happy for Michelle. But I was also very concerned. Whatever would my Christian friends and neighbours think? What would my mother think? My mind went through the numerous negative possibilities. Would they think I had 'converted' this unsuspecting young girl? Would they think I might try to do the same with them? Would they believe me if I said the choice was entirely her own, between her and God? I naïvely hoped that only Muslims would get to know of her decision.

Just a few weeks later, Michelle started wearing a headscarf. She also found a good smoking spot on the church path. My non-Muslim friends and neighbours found out pretty quickly. So did my mother.

Welcome to Islam

Nevertheless, my Muslim friends and I threw a celebratory party for Michelle at my home. Our older children stayed up for the occasion. I gave a short speech called 'Welcome to Islam'. Michelle then said her *shahadah*, the two-line summary of the Muslim faith, and along with two witnesses, she signed her 'Declaration of Faith' certificate. Each woman came up to Michelle, and gave her a warm embrace.

We went into the kitchen where Michelle noticed the chocolate cake, which had been inscribed by a friend with the word 'Congratulations'. While Michelle cut the cake, the children sang a song they had made up to the tune of 'Happy Birthday to you' – cunningly called 'Happy *shahadah* to you'. And the adults and children alike gathered around to enjoy the cake.

Our community was growing.

7 Community Spirit

'And do good unto ... the neighbour from among your own people, and the neighbour who is a stranger, and the friend by your side.'

(Qur'an 4:36)

'Your neighbour is forty houses ahead of you and forty houses at your back, forty houses to your left and forty houses to your right.'[1]

(Saying of Muhammad)

One of the reasons we had moved to Woking was that it was easy to leave it. There were fast rail links to London, a comprehensive bus network and easy access to motorways. An added benefit was that it had the mosque.

Woking mosque was the first purpose-built mosque not only in England but in the whole of north-west Europe, built in 1889. An English convert to Islam, William Abdullah Quilliam, had opened the UK's first mosque in Liverpool just a few months earlier but he had adapted a terrace house, so Woking could – and did – still claim to have the first mosque built specifically for prayer. Now nestled in well-tended private grounds between a retirement home and a DIY shop, Woking mosque looked like a haven of tranquillity, the perfect place to develop a sense of Muslim community.

Mothers meeting

I already had one friend in Woking before I arrived. Nasheeba was a British Muslim; her parents had come from Pakistan and our husbands had been friends at university. She was full of practical advice on a range of subjects including recipes, dentists and the summer sales. When I was pregnant for the first time, Nasheeba lent me her baby so I could practise bathing one before I had my own. And whenever I wasn't sure about a decision I was about to make, she always reminded me to turn to God and to ask Him for help.

Through Nasheeba, I had got to know other Muslim women in Woking who were all mothers of young children already. There was a bubbly Canadian called Farah whose parents also originated from Pakistan. There was Allia, also of Pakistani origins – the first friend I had ever had who wore a black *abaya* and a black scarf; the same friend who had lost her baby when heavily pregnant. And there was Saji – a Malaysian convert to Islam from Sikhism – who was working part-time at a local school.

We met up fortnightly during the day in each other's houses – over tea, coffee and lots of food. The preschoolers happily scattered bits of jigsaw and Lego all over the house. When it was time for prayer, we went to pray upstairs in turn, leaving the other women supervising all the toddlers so we could each pray in relative peace. We took our babies with us though: they lay on the floor while we prostrated over their little bodies, quickly thanking God for everything we had been given. At three o'clock, the house emptied within minutes, as those with school-age children rushed off to pick up their older children. And then the clear-up operation began.

I was in this routine when Julian's youngest brother Daniele temporarily came to stay, looking for a quiet place to study for upcoming exams. I warned him that a few women and children would be visiting the house – he wisely decided to stay upstairs. After three hours, he came down and surveyed the devastation. 'Are these your friends?' he asked. His own friends never left the place in such a mess. 'Yes,' I told him with a smile, 'These are my friends.'

Technically speaking

Although I did many of my prayers on my own or with friends at home, I still wanted to become involved in the mosque. The mosque was being inundated with calls from nearby primary schools. The Religious Education curriculum for two of the year groups included a detailed section on places of worship for Muslims: teachers were keen for the children to look around their local historical mosque. On the days when I was not working, I offered to help with giving the children a short tour; the mosque committee agreed.

In the original mosque building, I explained to the school children that the whole world was a mosque.[2] A mosque, or *masjid* in Arabic, literally meant a place of prostration. Muslims could pray anywhere. Two little children were clearly awake. 'Not the rubbish dump though,' said the first. Yes, probably not the rubbish dump. 'And not the toilet either', added the second, accompanied by fits of giggles from the children around him, who seemed to find any mention of toilets inordinately funny. They were right: Muslims could pray anywhere as long as it was clean. And if it was not clean, we could make a clean spot to pray by laying down a prayer mat. Or we could use a towel. A few times, I have used a scarf.

To comply with their syllabus, I pointed out the different parts of the mosque: the *minbar*, or pulpit, for the *imam* to deliver the weekly sermon, and the *mihrab*, a niche set in the wall, which showed the direction to pray towards Mecca, and therefore ultimately towards the Ka'bah. The school syllabus was focused on these technical terms but the reality was that Muslims didn't have to use either a *minbar* or a *mihrab* for prayer. Before performing the Friday prayer, an *imam* could simply stand up to talk, instead of talking from a pulpit. We did want to know which direction to face, and the *mihrab* showed us that – but, if we were not in a mosque, we could always work it out, use a compass, or ask someone who knew instead. And if we didn't know the direction, we should pray anyway (2:115).

A child's perspective

For the majority of children, it was their first time ever in a mosque. I asked if they had expected to see something different. 'Where are all the chairs?' asked one girl. I demonstrated that the way Muslims pray didn't require chairs: we pray so close to each other and need to be able to stand, bow down and then put our foreheads on the ground. Chairs would generally just get in the way, although I added that old and infirm people could pray sitting on chairs.

'Where are all the pictures?' asked one little boy, clearly more used to other houses of worship. The children began examining the windows, to see if they could decipher the shapes. 'They are all just stars,' observed his friend. He was right – the windows were decorated with a geometrical star-shaped pattern. I explained that no images of any living being were allowed in a mosque: Muslims don't want any distractions from worshipping God. And then their attention turned to the ceiling. I thought they might notice the ornate chandelier or the detailed Arabic calligraphy. An inquisitive girl spoke up. 'Why isn't that light bulb working?'

I read out some of the calligraphy on the ceilings and the walls. Around the *mihrab,* there was the whole of *Sura Fatihah*, starting with 'Praise be to God, the Most Kind, the Most Merciful.' I pointed to the words as I read them from right to left in Arabic before translating them to English. As I finished, a child asked me: 'Why do Muslims read backwards?'

On the way out of the mosque, one of the teachers drew the children's attention to the *wudu* area, where Muslims can wash before prayers if they are not already clean. It included two toilets: one 'Western-style' and one 'Eastern-style' squat toilet, bearing a strong resemblance to a hole in the ground. 'Look, children,' pointed out the teacher, 'A girl toilet and a boy toilet.'

Exposing the differences

While the children were busy sketching the mosque, the teachers took the opportunity to ask a few questions of their own. The first one was 'Why do you wear a scarf?' Then one lady asked me: 'Why do Muslims need to practise their prayers?' She mentioned she had seen Muslims pray in congregation, and before the prayer everyone had done a few actions on their own. The light dawned: she was talking about voluntary prayers. I explained that the short congregational prayer was compulsory but, before and after the prayer, people could choose to pray their own additional prayers to God. We had to practise memorizing the chapters of the Qur'an but we didn't need to practise our prayers.

The teacher's comment that struck me the most was the one relating to Asim, who had accompanied me that day. 'It's great for our children to see your child, to see him looking so normal', she said. She was trying to be complimentary but it did make me wonder. Had she really expected my little Muslim child to look so different to everyone else? What was 'normal' anyway? Nevertheless, I was glad she was happy.

Two months later, I was glad she had made the effort to come at all. Another primary school had arranged a date for a visit but then telephoned me to cancel. The teacher in charge of the proposed trip explained to me that objections by parents were so numerous that there were not enough children to make the trip worthwhile. Parents were concerned about what the children might be exposed to in a mosque and had withheld their permission for them to attend. I was disappointed. I wondered how these children were ever going to accept – let alone benefit from – the diversity within our British culture if they couldn't even be exposed to a different faith, for 30 minutes, in a supervised atmosphere. The teacher was equally disappointed and asked me to visit the school instead. I did my best to make it fun for the children, getting them to vote about the meaning of God and Allah, and getting them to dress up in 'Muslim clothes' from around the world, but I was sure the children would have much preferred the adventure of an outing to the mosque in a coach.

Committing to the committee

I was invited by two committee members – a local English convert named Khalil and a Pakistani Brigadier – to join the Mosque committee. I was keen to have input into the decisions and activities of the mosque. And the meetings were on a Sunday morning, meaning that Julian would be spending some quality time with his children. It seemed like a win-win situation, for me even if not necessarily for Julian.

When I joined the rest of the men at the meeting, there was some muttering in Urdu around me: the *imam* was asked for a *fatwa,* or opinion, about a woman being present. In Urdu, he decreed I could be at the meeting, but that I would have to move my chair back away from the rest of the group by 1 metre – the Brigadier translated for me. I thought it was a ridiculous ruling. But I complied.

We discussed the annual opening up of the mosque to the general public. It was primarily being organized by the police with the theme of community safety: it was going to be a fun day, with food stalls, a demonstration fire engine and free fairground rides. The mosque's role was to provide the venue and the free curry, which always went down well. But the *imam* was concerned about the money raised. 'Non-Muslim money can only be spent on the toilets,' he explained. I hadn't heard that in the Qur'an or the *hadith*. And I was intrigued about how he was going to physically separate the non-Muslim cash from the Muslim variety.

There was also discussion about the development of the mosque. The right-turn out of the mosque into the main road was dangerous, but the Head of the Mosque Committee had a proposal that would help. He suggested that women should not be allowed to turn right. I could just imagine asking the Council to design that particular sign. The conversation moved on to the new pathway being planned leading to the men's prayer hall: two men expressed concern that from an aerial view, the intersection of the pathway with the road leading to the car park would make a 'Christian cross' formation, which was clearly *haram*.

Making the right decision

Then Khalil initiated a debate about a children's playground that the Council had agreed to fund for the local people, within the mosque grounds. Khalil asked me to show a proposed layout that a professional playground designer had produced, to show the rest of the committee the kind of thing that could be done. But the committee was not impressed. Would that mean there would be non-Muslims on the premises? What if the women were inappropriately dressed? And would the springy animal-shaped equipment have eyes, suggesting representation of living beings within the grounds of the mosque? The *imam* suggested postponing any decision on the playground until later.

I was frustrated with the *imam*. Like many of the *imams* in the UK, he was not familiar with the British culture – or the language. I wanted an English-speaking *imam*, ideally one trained in the UK. But everyone's expectations for the *imam* were so high: ideally he would be fluent in Arabic and Urdu as well as English; he would have a thorough grounding in Islamic knowledge; and he would have the organizational decision-making and teaching skills to run a *madrasa*, an Islamic supplementary school for children. He would also have the personality to connect with the Muslim community locally as well as external entities such as schools and the police. Yet, despite the high demands, the salary on offer was so low. Unsurprisingly, there were never many applicants from the UK.

I came back from the committee meeting at 1.30pm to find Asim climbing up his high chair, desperate for food. 'I have no idea what he wants,' Julian said.

Woking mosque eventually appointed a new *imam*: he was from South Africa. In addition to speaking Arabic and Urdu, he was fluent in English. The mosque had lost the playground funding due to inaction, but it was still making progress. And the council put up a road sign indicating that no one was allowed to turn right out of the mosque – not even the men.

Celebrating the Jubilee

Julian and I also got involved in our street committee for the Queen's Jubilee Party. Well it was strictly a half a street committee: the road was a long one so we agreed we would only invite people who lived to the left of the post box. It also wasn't to be held on the street: with the English weather being so unpredictable we held the event at the church on our road.

Committee meetings were quick and action focused. Everybody was helpful, volunteering to sell tickets, book a band, make the cake, plan the food and decorate the hall – and then they carried out what they had undertaken to do. Jonathan, one of my churchgoing neighbours on the committee, discovered a straightforward form enabling us to apply for a Council grant for up to £250 towards the cost of the party. As the Treasurer, I filled it in. I went with Jonathan's wife Helen and our small children to hand it to the Council; we were awarded the full grant just a few days later. Tickets were expensive but people paid willingly. And the whole event made a profit, which went to a shelter up the road for abused women.

The high level of organization I found among these English

Christians made it so easy to get things done. Safiyya had told me: 'Mummy, I wish I was Muslim on the inside but Christian on the outside.' Sometimes I wished I was too.

Neighbourly spirit

The children and I enjoyed getting to know the fellow members on the Jubilee committee neighbours on a more social level.

My immediate neighbour, Barbara, was a kind and committed member of the local church whose own children had just left home. Over cups of tea in my kitchen, she offered me comforting stories about her own children while I was battling with mine. And we talked about the struggle mothers have to maintain a career while looking after the family. I apologized for the noise and the chaos that permanently seemed to surround our conversations.

Then just before Christmas time, Barbara took all of the children while I delivered chocolates to other neighbours. I arrived back after five minutes to find noise and chaos in her home too. Asim was covered in blood, Amaani had scratches, and Safiyya was vehemently denying she had anything to do with it. Asim had somehow got wrapped up in Barbara's Christmas tree, the needles of the tree had pierced his skin, and he had clutched onto little Amaani for help, bringing her down with him. Barbara looked frazzled.

I appreciated the effort that Barbara made to be an integral part of the children's life. But it wasn't unreciprocated – by inviting themselves over to 'help' in her garden and harass the fish, the children made very sure that they remained involved in hers.

Paradise on the beach

Helen generously invited me to take a day trip to the seaside with her own young family using public transport. It was a busy day, dragging the babies and toddlers on and off buses and trains, and chasing them as they chased the seagulls and threw pebbles into the freezing water. Helen's husband Jonathan was indispensable, helping with pushchairs and sleeping infants and making sure we were catching the right train in the right direction. It was a relief for us all to escape our child-centred suburban lifestyle for the day. As the day was drawing to an end we managed to grab a few minutes of adult conversation.

The conversation turned to religion, specifically their religion, evangelical Christianity. As we negotiated pedestrian crossings and grabbed wayward toddlers, Jonathan explained how we were all born full of sin due to our ancestor Adam and that we could not approach God directly due to our sinful state. We had to go via an intermediary – all prayers must therefore be through Jesus Christ. I asked many questions about their belief and what they believed about others. Eventually, Jonathan was forced to tell me he thought I was going straight to Hell. But he was very apologetic. And he said it in a very nice way.

The Bible says: 'Jesus answered him: I am the way, the truth and the life. No one goes to the Father except through me' (John 14:6). I knew about that verse: I had learned it by heart at Sunday school. But I believed in Jesus too: Muslims could not be Muslims unless they believed in Jesus and the miracles within his birth, life and death. I believed Jesus, like his mother Mary, was not only born completely innocent but protected from sin throughout life (3:35–36). But I didn't believe Jesus was God – or that I had to pray to Jesus to get to God. I was also not convinced that I was going to Hell: I had no idea where I was going – or where Jonathan and Helen were going either. I believed God would, with infinite Mercy, judge us all.

Helen was convinced that, for as long as I remained Muslim, our paths could never cross in the next life. Fortunately, we were both happy to see more of each other in this one.

Breaking up the party

Pauline had children who were of a similar age to mine. Pauline lived over the road, just a few houses away – we had originally met in the church hall at Bethany Babes but now often got together after school for tea. She was an irreverent and straight-speaking 'northerner', married to a man whose mother was from Holland and whose father was a Sikh from India. Pauline was always very hospitable; her house was typically filled with people. And so when she held a first birthday party for her son, the children and I went along to join in the fun.

I was in the kitchen chatting with Pauline and a couple of other mothers about children and after-school activities when her father-in-law came in and started a conversation with me on a completely different topic. He said to me accusingly: 'You are a Muslim. Why do you hate Sikhs?' The other mums promptly left the kitchen to continue their conversation. Pauline's father-in-law then told me how many of his friends been killed by Muslims in 1947. He was talking about the mass movement of Muslims, Hindus and Sikhs in the British-orchestrated Partition between Pakistan and India. The violence was on all sides: hundreds of thousands of Muslims were killed too. Regardless, I had nothing to do with it. I hadn't even been born then. Thankfully, Pauline came back in and saw what was happening – she called me upstairs 'to have a look at something'. I had been rescued.

The final journey

Life was busy and happy but, in the back of my mind, I knew it was all only temporary: as it said in the Qur'an: 'Every human being is bound to taste death' (3:185). I had never been to a Muslim funeral. I didn't know what I would need to do spiritually and practically, either to prepare for the death of a Muslim in my family or to prepare for my own. And so when the Islamic Foundation in Leicester offered a course for converts to Islam on the subject, I was quick to sign up. 'That's very morbid, Lucy, why would you want to spend your weekend there?' asked Pauline, the day before I went.

The course was called 'the Final Journey' and covered everything to do with dying, including the Islamic view of death and the separation of the soul from the body as well as practical arrangements: making a will, washing the body and the funeral itself. We learnt how to shroud others as if for burial – and we were prepared ourselves.

I lay on the table in the conference room unable to move, wrapped up in layers of white sheets, without my watch, without my glasses and without even my wedding ring. The closest experience I could relate to this was when I had a hospital operation requiring general anaesthetic: I had been dressed in a white hospital gown, stripped of any accessories and left in a room on my own, waiting for my turn. It vividly brought home to me that, on the Day of Judgement, all my possessions would be left behind. I would only have those actions that outlived me but lived on through others and my absolute faith in God.

Scholarly advice

When we had taken off our white sheets, a respected Islamic scholar arrived to answer our questions. Sheikh al-Judai clarified that a Muslim may attend a non-Muslim funeral, and that a non-Muslim could attend the funeral of a Muslim, as well as help with the shrouding and the burial. He explained that organ donation in order to sustain life was allowed from the living or the dead, unless a dead person had explicitly withheld permission while alive. And he emphasized the need to respect and give life to the living, while also treating the dead with care.

One convert asked the scholar about the practice of some people living in Britain who flew bodies 'back home' to be buried. The scholar gave a *fatwa* that this was acceptable. Then the questioner explained that the body was prepared for transport through injection with a combination of formaldehyde and ethanol. And ethanol was also known as alcohol. Sheikh al-Judai didn't hesitate: on the basis of the new information, he changed his *fatwa*, and declared it unislamic. I knew a *fatwa* was only an opinion: different people had different opinions. As I had just witnessed, even a single scholar can have several different opinions – within a very short space of time.[3]

Our time is up

I got back home late Sunday evening. On Monday morning, Pauline rang the doorbell, and stood in the doorway: she had some shocking news to give me. Her husband had died of a sudden heart attack, in the early hours of that morning while travelling with his colleagues on his way to work. Our families had got together for Sunday lunch only the previous week. Pauline was now left alone to bring up their two young children. I couldn't believe it.

Members of the church community, neighbours and friends all rallied around Pauline as best as we could, feeding her children, contacting authorities and making lots of cups of tea. But nothing could or would ever replace her husband Ravi. I went to the funeral service, held in a church and listened to the eulogy. From God we come and to God we return.

Six months later, I went to my first funeral service in a mosque, the funeral of my friend Somia's father. I now knew that in Islam, unlike in English culture, it was respectful to rush to bury the body. And so after the funeral, while I stayed with the children, Julian went quickly to the graveyard. Everyone present took turns to cover her father's coffin with three handfuls of soil, saying the words Muhammad had spoken: 'From it did we create you, to it shall we return you, and from it shall we bring you forth another time.'[4] It was a simple service and a simple burial. All that was left was a mound of earth, with a marker on top. From God we come and to God we return.

A life barely begun

And then, only a few weeks afterwards, I found myself at another Muslim funeral. It was for the much-wanted baby girl of my Canadian Muslim friend, Farah. The funeral of Amaara was made even more poignant for me as Farah and I had both been pregnant at the same time – and I was now there at the funeral with my living baby, and she was there without hers. Little Amaara had died while still in hospital, at only seven days old. Despite the death of her baby, Farah found her body was still being affected by the changes that happen naturally to all new mothers: her milk had 'come in' ready for her to breastfeed, providing a physical and upsetting reminder of the birth she had just been through.

Then the coffin was brought into the mosque. It was tiny. The women – and the men – couldn't hold back their tears.

On the way back from Amaara's funeral, Safiyya calmly analysed the situation. 'That baby died because her big sisters didn't teach her how to breathe. Asim is alive because I taught him.' I couldn't believe it: the last thing anyone in that family needed was to feel any guilt. I told her that only God decides who will live and who will die. Big sisters had little to do with it.

For Farah, the pain was clearly deep: not only physically but also mentally and emotionally. It helped a huge amount that she believed – as did we all – that it was God's will. Farah held on to her faith, using it to help her cope not only with the funeral but with the many difficult months afterwards. I saw her emerge a stronger person from the experience. Eventually she left to make a new life for herself, her husband and her other children 'back home' with her parents in Canada. I knew it couldn't have been easy. From God we come and to God we return.

Kitchen politics

Pauline and I now met frequently: Julian was away due to his work much of the time and her husband was now away all the time. We fed each other's children, enjoyed noisy Sunday lunches together, and talked about life. We only had one argument: it was about whether we should go to war in Iraq.

From what I had gleaned simply from scouring the *Guardian* and the *Independent* newspapers, it seemed highly probable that Iraq didn't have chemical and nuclear capability. Pauline thought that Iraq did have the weapons, given that the UK had been involved in supplying them to Iraq in the 1980s in the first place. Yet now the weapons inspectors could not find any evidence of weapons-usable nuclear material and most of the chemical weapons development complex had been dismantled.

The main outstanding issue seemed to be biological weapons: in 1995, Saddam Hussein's son-in-law had defected and admitted destroying all biological weapons but Iraq's disclosures about these weapons were incomplete and inaccurate. Our leading politicians were therefore convinced that Iraq continued to hide large quantities of biological agents. Yet I thought it was quite possible Iraq might just have some very bad accounting systems – or some very bad accountants.[5] Chief weapons Inspector Hans Blix had also found that some of Iraq's ballistic missiles could travel up to 50 km beyond the 150 km limit set by the UN. Less than two weeks later, Iraq had[6] begun to destroy them as ordered but some missiles remained.

I didn't see why we needed to declare war, even if Iraq did have a missile range that included weapons capable of travelling up to 200 km. Russia was testing a ballistic missile with a range of over 10,000 km[7] – should we invade them? Other countries outside the Nuclear Non-proliferation Treaty were also suspected of having nuclear weapons, including Israel and Pakistan – should we invade them too? Other countries were run by unelected leaders; other countries were engaged in human rights abuses – should we invade them too?

Whatever happened to dialogue and discussion and peaceful containment? And if we occupied another country, thousands of innocent people would inevitably die as 'collateral damage' – what about them? Over a hundred billion barrels of proven oil reserves[8] in Iraq could be affecting our leaders' judgement.

Tony Blair seemed personally convinced the war would be a war fought for justice, freedom and democracy. For him, it would be a just war. Like Blair, Pauline thought we needed to go ahead, albeit for rather different reasons – she hoped he might be a moderating influence on the US. Like Blair, I believed in just wars, but I didn't think this war was one of them. I couldn't convince Pauline and she couldn't convince me. We were both very angry. Not even several cups of strong tea could calm the tension in my kitchen.

Going to war

Julian and I took our young children to the demonstration march in London, where we walked alongside hundreds of thousands of others. There were Muslims, Christians, Socialist Workers, politicians, men, women and children. Some of my mother's friends were there – they ended up marching among a group of Muslims. One woman was holding a placard saying 'Make tea, not war'.

Despite our protests, the UK and the US decided to occupy Iraq. It was an expensive decision – on many fronts. Julian was so angry he kicked a football across our kitchen and it broke one of our wedding presents, a hand-painted fruit bowl. I replaced the bowl; the war was unaffected.

Three months after the war began, Julian came back from work and emptied his work backpack in the kitchen. He brought out a translation of the Qur'an, a book called *The No-nonsense Guide to Islam*[9] and a map of Iraq. I knew he had been on a team-building activity for the day – I asked him what was going on. 'We went clay-pigeon shooting,' he explained, 'And I won.' That didn't surprise me:

at school, he had always been a good marksman. He added: 'These were my prizes.' He told me that the department secretary now felt terrible: 'I don't know what I was thinking of when I chose these presents,' she had told him when she saw he was the winner. 'I had thought it would be funny.' Julian added the books to our collection, kept the map of Iraq, and took his rucksack back to work.

Feeling suicidal

And then in 2005, four British Muslims decided to change everything. London came to a standstill; 52 people lost their lives in the first suicide bombings in Western Europe. The impact of the bombings reverberated across the UK and over the globe. The impact was felt in Woking.

I was teaching in a classroom at the time just as news was filtering out. One of my pupils was in tears. She didn't know where her father was; she just knew he worked in London. Her friend comforted her, while I tried to focus the attention of the rest of the class back on to the subject of algebra. I felt guilty: some of my coreligionists had done this, and now I was trying to brush it aside. But I just didn't want everyone to panic.

The following day, the newspapers reported that the ringleader was working in a school as a mentor; he was also involved in a youth club. That was very disturbing news. Already, any British Muslim who was not 'integrated' into the wider community was a potential suspect for terrorist activity. But now a British Muslim could be 'integrated', working in a school and involved in community work, and still be a potential suicide bomber and a justifiable focus of suspicion. I hoped I was wrong. Anyway, from a personal perspective I expected I would be fine. I had known my neighbours for years.

I soon sensed the atmosphere had subtly changed: my usual trips to the town centre generated stares; Lena was being given deadly looks in her village by little old ladies emerging out of Boots the

Chemist; a Muslim friend in Woking came to me in tears after having been accused of having a bomb under her scarf and another was chased down the street. My neighbours did not seem to be quite as friendly as usual. Julian and his fellow Muslim commuters stopped carrying their rucksacks.

Justifying war

Barbara's husband Chris approached me and asked me to arrange for a few of my Muslim friends and acquaintances to meet with a group of people who lived on and around my street, to help them start to make sense of what had happened. The neighbours wanted to know about *jihad* and suicide bombing. My friend Zahra, a local optometrist, clarified the 'Muslim position'.

I did wonder why Zahra had to explain what other Muslims were doing in the name of God. All the leaders believed God was on their side. Tony Blair had prayed to God over Iraq; God had apparently even told George Bush: 'George, go and end the tyranny in Iraq.' Yet I wouldn't dream of presuming that those neighbours who firmly held on to the Christian faith were in any way associated with the loss of innocent life caused by the British- and American-led armies. Anyway, I was happy that my neighbours thought there was room for discussion. They listened intently.

'Islam is clear,' Zahra told them. 'Suicide is prohibited. It says in the Qur'an: "Do not kill yourselves, for truly God has been to you Most Merciful" (4:29).[10] And killing of innocent people is also prohibited. The Qur'an says: "If anyone slays a human being – unless it be (in punishment) for murder or for spreading corruption on earth – it shall be as though he had slain all mankind; whereas, if anyone saves a life, it shall be as though he had saved the lives of all mankind"'(5:32). Zahra explained that killing people who were just getting on with their daily lives was categorically outside Islam. I could see my neighbours relax a little: they were clearly comforted that the Muslims around them didn't believe in random bombings.

I had noticed that *jihad* was usually translated in the press as 'Holy War', conjuring up associations of spreading Islam violently and punishing the 'infidels'. But I knew *jihad* came from the Arabic word *jahada*, meaning 'to strive' – it appeared frequently in the Qur'an meaning 'to strive in the way of God'. There were two kinds of *jihad* mentioned: the greater *jihad* and the lesser *jihad*. The greater and more difficult *jihad* was the struggle to improve oneself and society,[11] through the heart, the tongue, the pen and the hand. But then there was the lesser *jihad*: the struggle against oppression and injustice.

The main British Muslim bomber Khan had declared in a video statement that he was dying for Islam, in the path of *jihad*.

The innocent die

The Qur'an did permit fighting in self-defence and for the protection of family and property (22:39–40). I had asked my mother whether she thought my father would sit back if someone attempted to come in and take over or obliterate the family home: she immediately replied: 'He wouldn't let that happen easily.' I understood: it seemed only natural to fight back. But even if fighting was for self-defence, or for protection, Khan seemed to have forgotten that in Islam there was no justification ever for killing the innocent by any method (5:32) – including suicide bombing.

Suicide bombing wasn't actually a 'Muslim issue'. In July 2005, the month of the British bombings, the *American Conservative* magazine had interviewed a Chicago Professor, Robert Pape, who had documented every suicide-terrorist attack from 1980 to 2004 and unearthed some interesting facts.[12] The world leaders in suicide-terrorism were the Tamil Tigers, a secular Marxist group from Hindu families in Sri Lanka – they invented the suicide vest. The Professor also found that 95 per cent of all incidents had the central objective of compelling a democratic state to withdraw from occupying land that was not theirs. They were fighting back.

Al-Qaida have claimed responsibility for numerous bombings. But elected governments have taken actions – including the launch of cluster bombs and deployment of armies into heavily populated areas – which have also resulted in the deaths of unarmed men, women and children. The intentions may have been different but the end result is that the innocent have died. It reminded me of the African proverb: 'When two elephants fight, it is the grass that gets trampled.'

Don't panic

An Irishman at our little gathering lightened the sombre mood by empathizing with our unpopular status. 'I used to keep my mouth firmly shut on the London Underground in the 1970s,' he told us, 'so that no-one would realize I was Irish and start to panic. But at least I was white: if I didn't talk, I blended in.' He looked around at the scarves covering up the hair of some of the women and the darker colouring of some of the Muslims in the group and continued: 'It's a shame you Muslims can't do the same.'

At the end of the meeting, Chris asked us: 'What can we do to make life easier for you Muslims?' It was a generous question. I responded hopefully: 'It would be great if you could just learn to trust us again.' His response was honest yet distressing. 'It's not that easy,' he replied. 'It will take time.' I went home for a cup of tea. If I wasn't Muslim, I would have drunk something stronger. But then, if I wasn't Muslim, many things would have been very different.

8 Fasting and Feasting

'O you who have attained to faith! Fasting is ordained for you as it was ordained for those before you, so that you might remain conscious of God.'

(Qur'an 2:183)

'Be mindful of God and God will protect you. Be mindful of God and you will find him before you. If you ask, ask of God. If you seek help, seek help of God.'[1]

(Saying of Muhammad)

Back in 1992, my first Ramadan was approaching. I always had three meals a day. An additional but firm fixture on my student timetable was four o'clock tea and biscuits. How would I ever manage?

Preparing for Ramadan

I knew how Ramadan was meant to work: the guidelines surrounding fasting in Islam were the same across the globe.[2] From dawn to sunset, Muslims would be abstaining from food, drink, smoking, and sexual relations. For the whole month, I would have to get up very early to eat a pre-dawn meal; after the short dawn prayer called *Fajr*, I could stay up to pray some more and read, or I could go back to sleep. Then I was meant to continue normal daily activities without food or drink, while in a heightened state of spirituality. At sunset, I would be able to eat again. I could eat whatever food I wanted but – like Muslims across the world – I would have to start with a few dates. I had never eaten dates before, although I used to enjoy fig biscuits.

In Ramadan, there was also a lot of extra prayer involved. In addition to the five compulsory prayers a day there was a Ramadan-specific voluntary prayer called *tarawih* in the evenings; at other times of day or night, Muslims should be striving to fit further voluntary prayers and Qur'an reading into their regular routine. And then on top of all that hunger, thirst, praying and reading, Muslims were meant to be giving generously both to charity and to neighbours. I could see this month was going to be a major challenge.

Ramadan was meant to bring major benefits too. After 29 or 30 days of fasting, I should have developed a heightened awareness of God, a renewed empathy towards the less fortunate, an improved focus on prayer, and an increase in my level of knowledge about Islam. I should also have learnt self-restraint – both in tucking into chocolate biscuits and in putting on the kettle.

Tired and hungry

Ramadan didn't get off to an auspicious start. 'Come with us to Leicester,' urged my student Muslim friends, embarking on a Friday night escapade out of university to the Islamic Foundation for the weekend. 'It will be fun' they assured me, 'And you'll really feel the spirit of Ramadan.' I went. It was a political conference called 'When the Sun rises from the West': my friends had a different idea of fun from me.

On the Saturday morning, I appeared in the breakfast hall at 4am as instructed. Everyone was tucking into platefuls of curry and rice; there was no cereal in sight. So I helped myself to what was on offer. It certainly made a change from my usual bowl of bran flakes. The other students were full of energy and the room was buzzing with conversation. And then the chocolate appeared. The girls passed it around; everyone was eating it. I hesitated: I loved chocolate but wondered if I could really stomach it at this early hour. I gave into peer pressure but it was a bad idea – by 7am, I was ravenous. I had eaten such a big breakfast that my stomach had expanded in anticipation of more food.

I spent most of the time at the Islamic Foundation feeling very hungry. Muhammad said: 'Many people who fast will gain nothing from their fast but hunger and thirst'.[3] I was fitting into that category. I went to sleep during a lot of the talks to try to make the hunger pangs go away. Then, in the evening, the *tarawih* prayers started. I was still finding it an achievement to pray five times a day, and this *tarawih* prayer was an exhausting 90-minute prayer marathon. It was a relief to get back to university.

Student efforts

At college, I scaled down my expectations, focusing on my own personal Ramadan target of simply abstaining completely from all food and drink. I soon learnt that fasting became much easier if I ate only a light breakfast; it also gave me a few more minutes in bed. Then, once I was up, I appreciated those quiet hours in the early morning to complete my essays that always had to be handed in by 9am. On essay-free days, I dipped into my translation of the Qur'an. I discovered verses about topics that ranged from washing one's face (5:6) to inheritance law (4:11-12; 4:176) and from being fair in business (11:84-88) to life in the Hereafter (many). The days went by: each day, I was delighted that I had survived the fast.

A PhD student came to interview me for her thesis about women who had become Muslim. She had so many questions to ask; I was getting thirsty. I grabbed some water and then carried on where I had left off, which happened to be explaining the intricacies of

Ramadan. And then I realized I had just broken my fast – even as I was talking about it. I was mortified. But I wasn't the only person in history to have done it. Muhammad said: 'Whoever forgot while he was fasting and ate or drank he should complete his fast, for it was God who fed him.'[4] I mentally thanked God for feeding – or, rather, watering – me. I explained what had happened to the rather bewildered researcher; I carried on my fast.

Finding out about fasting

The economics students at my college soon noticed I was up to something as I no longer met up for chats over mugs of tea. I explained that I was fasting each day until sunset and so all daytime tea and biscuits were temporarily out of bounds. 'Do you think you will lose weight?' asked one girl, sensing a potential dieting opportunity. I told her that was definitely not meant to be the purpose behind it – and anyway, if I ate lots of chocolate at four o'clock in the morning I was more than likely to put it on. Another thought it was excessive that I couldn't even drink water in daylight hours: 'How are you going to manage?' she asked, incredulously. I knew a billion Muslims over the world coped with it, the majority in much hotter climates than in the UK and it wasn't as if I was a prolific water-drinker. Anyway, I had been fasting for two weeks already and I was still alive.

But there was one critical question that all the students wanted to know the answer to: what do Muslims do on the North Pole? It was a question that wasn't very relevant to my life – and even less relevant to theirs – but they wanted the answer anyway. So I went away to find out.

I reported back to my inquisitive peer group that the Saudis had issued a *fatwa* on this very subject.[5] Even if there wasn't a massive Muslim community living at the North Pole, the issue of non-stop daylight did genuinely affect Muslims in northern Norway, Finland

and Alaska. The Saudis had decreed that in countries where it was not possible to distinguish day from night, Muslims should follow the timetable of the nearest country where the sun sets. I accepted that would still mean a very long day of fasting for those in the North Pole. Maybe they should consider moving south for a little while.

Two girls volunteered to fast with me for a day: Sriya, my Hindu friend with whom I had enjoyed long discussions about religion, and Annabelle, an economics student from Zimbabwe. 'I want to see what it is like,' Annabelle said. 'I'm happy to keep you both company,' offered Sriya. I appreciated the support and told them the times they would need to start and finish fasting. We agreed that the three of us would fast in unison the following day and meet up to compare notes over dinner.

I popped in to Annabelle's room an hour before the end of the fast to see how she was doing. She confessed she had just had a cup of tea. I empathized: I would have found it difficult to give up food and drink completely for a day without an exceptionally good reason. Sriya was more disciplined: fasting was common in her Hindu faith and her own mother fasted frequently. At sunset, Sriya cooked a vegetarian meal for us and we all celebrated our efforts.

Giving up?

As a teenager, I frequently used to observe Lent by attempting to 'give up' a favourite foodstuff for 40 days. But I could never manage it: I enjoyed chocolate biscuits too much. The only time I was successful was when I gave up rice pudding – which I couldn't stand at any time of year. If anything, I was too successful: other school-friends caught on to the idea and gave the dessert up too. Before long, the school dinner ladies started protesting about the quantities of rice pudding that were not being eaten and a decree was issued that we were not allowed to 'give up' any of the school food for Lent. It was very disappointing. For me, once again, Lent became an insurmountable challenge.

I was amazed that I found Ramadan easier. It was easier because at sunset each day I could drink and eat whatever I liked – including tea and chocolate biscuits. There was no sense of long-term deprivation. It was easier because I knew that there was a worldwide community of people all doing the same thing – even if I didn't see much of them it was reassuring to know I was not alone. But the main reason it was easier was because I believed that, now I was Muslim, it was compulsory. I simply couldn't eat or drink during the day. There was no point stressing about it, or getting tempted, or having even a sip of tea: I just had to get on with it. And in the process, I discovered a mental strength I never knew I had.

Reasons to celebrate

The textbooks had told me that the month of Ramadan was immediately followed by the day of *Eid ul Fitr* – the Festival of Breaking the Fast – a time of great celebration. Everyone would be getting new clothes; there would be a special prayer at the mosque and people would gather with families and friends to enjoy a vast array of food from whatever culture they wanted. It sounded fun.

The day of *Eid* arrived but it wasn't fun. It was just another day. I tried to find some Muslims to share it with and soon discovered most Muslim students had gone back to their families to celebrate *Eid* with them. I knew there was a mosque somewhere in town but wasn't too sure how to get to it. No one else in college was aware that it was a day of any significance. Christmas seemed infinitely better – and also impossible to miss.

I loved Christmas. But now I was Muslim – and Muslims didn't seem to celebrate it. As we packed up our student rooms to prepare for the upcoming holidays with our families, the girl living in the room next door said to me: 'You shouldn't be having Christmas. It's not as if you believe in Jesus, is it?'

Actually, I did believe in Jesus, I just wasn't keen on celebrating his birthday – regardless of whether or not it fell on 25 December. Many Muslims didn't celebrate Muhammad's birthday either. Many Muslims didn't even make a big deal about their own birthday – or the birthday of their children. I could see the advantage of that latter decision: all those party packs and games and children running around looked completely exhausting.

But I still wanted to celebrate on 25 December. I loved the whole occasion. It was the one time in the year when my extended family always made an effort to get together and so there were usually around 12 of us living under one roof for several days and nights. I also looked forward to the special dishes my mother made, the fairy lights, the evening carols, the tree decorations, the feature-length films on television, Father Christmas – and the presents. Especially as a child, presents were the main focus. And even now my sister was an adult, once people found out that her birthday was also on 25 December they still asked her, 'Do you get two lots of presents?'

I went home for my first Christmas as a Muslim, I took part in the celebrations and I bought everyone presents. I received them too. A small china Father Christmas sat on the dinner table and he had a few more individually labelled presents in his sack. As always, it was great fun.

Ramadan holidays

By the time it was my third Ramadan, I was living in London and ensconced in the workplace. I broke fast on the train home or – if working late – at the office. My colleagues were very understanding. If anything they were too understanding.

The Financial Manager held a presentation for all the analysts in the conference room with a buffet lunch beforehand. Due to the fast, I was invited to come after the lunch; the manager said she would explain to the others why I was coming later. I walked in to find the food thoughtfully covered up with a tablecloth, to ensure I wasn't tempted by the lavish offerings. The only problem was that I wasn't fasting that day.

The first time I had heard that women were ever exempt from religious duties was when my student friend and prayer teacher Sabiha had told me she was 'on holiday'. But she wasn't on holiday: she was right there, with me. Sabiha explained that, as a mercy from God, during their periods women didn't need to pray or fast. While the prayers never had to be made up, Sabiha explained that we would not be fasting any less than the men: we would have to fast some other time to make up for those we had missed, preferably before the next Ramadan came along.

And now I was 'on holiday' – and I didn't want to advertise the fact to the entire department. I sat through the meeting, eyeing the tablecloth. At the end, the Financial Manager prepared a plate of nibbles for me to eat 'later': I found a quiet office and ate it all sooner rather than later.

On other 'fasting-free' days in Ramadan, I went to the staff canteen hoping that people who saw me eating would be unaware it was Ramadan. They usually were.

Awareness of time

I developed mixed feelings about Ramadan. At the start of each day, I counted the hours until I could eat again. I missed not being able to grab a drink whenever I wanted. But I loved the feeling of calmness that fasting brought about, the constant awareness of what I was doing and the unusual opportunity to practise self-restraint. And the sensation of being able to eat and drink again at sunset was unbeatable.

My parents came back from a trip to Ethiopia, where the government was telling the Christian populace that they must fast every other day. The people followed the government's instruction: food was scarce – they had little choice. My mother recounted how she watched the teenagers lolling about with no energy – at the end of their fast there was little prospect of food. I knew that I was experiencing such a small hardship compared to them.

Yet at the weekends, the hours went by slowly. For the whole month, I kept away from the cinema, television and coffee shops. I knew Ramadan was the month to focus on increasing my acts of worship, so I tried to use my free time to read and understand the Qur'an in English, and to find other ways to learn more about my faith.

I went back to the Central Mosque in London's Regent's Park and joined Brother Brian's circle. Brother Brian was an elderly English gentleman who ran a Sunday study circle primarily for converts to Islam. Brother Brian asked an open question: 'What are we meant to make a special effort to do more of in Ramadan – and what should we do less of?' A man in the group volunteered various positive actions, including helping the poor directly and through donations, reading the Qur'an, sharing food, and remembering God. I decided to become involved. 'We shouldn't be getting angry, or lying, or spending time watching rubbish on television,' I proffered. 'But you shouldn't be doing any of those things anyway,' explained Brother Brian. I kept my mouth firmly closed for the rest of the session.

Calling centre

Aishah, the grown-up daughter of two English converts to Islam, kept me busy by involving me in a Ramadan fundraising drive for a charity called Islamic Relief. She told me it would be aired on Sunrise Radio, a radio station that was very popular among all British Asian listeners – Hindu, Sikh and Muslim.

The donations came flooding in and I was merely one of the many volunteers recording people's pledges. It took ages: people wanted to dedicate their voluntary donations to their nieces and nephews, uncles and aunts, and numerous other relatives. I had to record it diligently so that their largesse could be announced on the radio. One lady wanted 50p split between her eighteen grandchildren – it was a sweet thought that took an inordinate amount of time to process. This whole system of dedication was new to me: for Muslims, just as for Christians,[6] giving was ideally meant to be so discreet that the left hand didn't even know what the right hand was doing.

The Indian and Pakistani surnames I came across were new to me too. There was one caller whose surname I was finding particularly hard to grasp. I asked him to repeat it one last time. I wrote it down carefully and then I looked at what I had written. It said 'R U N Asian'. That was an unusual surname. And then the penny dropped: he was now asking me if I was an Asian – and he wanted to be passed on to someone who was. I had tried my best but it wasn't good enough – he wanted someone who could understand him better. I resolved to be a little less frustrated next time I phoned my local bank branch and got diverted to India, where call centre assistants often found it difficult to spell my surname. I passed the donor on to someone who spoke perfect Urdu.

Season of goodwill

My mother found out that Muslims had no choice about giving away 2.5 per cent of our savings a year, to fulfil the pillar of Islam known as *zakah*. She was concerned 'Who do they make you give it to?' she asked me.

Zakah literally meant 'purity': this compulsory charity was required to purify our wealth, purify our hearts from selfishness and purify the recipient's heart from envy. Most Muslims choose to donate their entire amount for the year in the month of Ramadan, the month when goodwill and good deeds are emphasized.

My mother and I talked about how this compulsory giving worked in England. I tried to assure her that there was no 'they'. 'I can give to any charity I want, in England or overseas. No one collects it centrally,' I explained. She had noticed that I occasionally received mail from Islamic Relief: I mentioned that this was an international charity that worked on behalf of all the world's poor, like the Red Cross, and the Catholic Agency Cafod. And I told her that the only organizations monitoring what we gave were the Inland Revenue – who kindly added on tax relief – and Julian's company, which generously doubled employee donations to recognized non-religious charities – including our donations to Islamic Relief. I could never be completely certain that my donation was ending up in the hands of those who needed it most but then that was a problem with any charitable giving – to any charity.

Going to celebrate

For *Eid*, Julian and I took the morning off work, put on some smart clothes and headed to Regent's Park mosque. Most of our fellow Underground users seemed oblivious to the occasion – I tried to imagine Christmas passing by in the same way. But by the time we were nearing the right station for the mosque, we had been joined by dozens of children and adults, all dressed up in their best attire. As we approached the mosque itself, we found the road congested with cars; police were directing traffic and there were hundreds of people now thronging the pavements alongside us. The sense of excitement was palpable.

Eid prayers were being repeated hourly – it looked like we had joined the mid-morning prayer time 'rush hour'. Julian and I split up. I headed to the women's section. I was relieved that I could go to the child-free area – the larger women's prayer hall was seething with children. The *Eid* prayer was slightly different from the usual ritual prayers: I copied the women next to me and hoped they knew what they were doing.

After the prayer I exchanged greetings and hugs with the unknown women whom I had been praying beside. They were a diverse group including Somalis, Arabs, Pakistanis and Bengalis as well as other English people; several had brought plates of treats to share after the prayers. The atmosphere was very different from the English Christmas church services I had grown up with, both in terms of the cultural diversity and the noise levels but it was an overwhelmingly warm and happy one.

Nevertheless, my *Eid* couldn't compete with Christmas, which remained an unmissable event in the calendar. I wrapped up presents to give to my relatives at Christmas time. This was my family's time to receive – and to give – gifts and I was part of the family. Julian and I even gave gifts to each other: it was hard to let go of these childhood traditions.

Season's greetings

Safiyya was born four months before my sixth Ramadan. That Ramadan was also going to coincide with Christmas for the first time in around 30 years. I was going to have to talk about this with my parents.

'But I thought Ramadan was in February,' said my mother, when I broached the subject. It was, and then it moved to January. Now it was in December. I attempted to provide a convincing explanation: 'Well, it is because the Islamic months are based on a lunar calendar, which is 11 days shorter than our solar Gregorian one. It therefore looks like Ramadan moves 11 days earlier each year but in fact it just operates on a different timetable.' I thought my mother might think that Muslims following the rhythms of the moon were living in a bygone era and so I added in a benefit: 'This way we get to experience Ramadan across all the seasons.' I considered mentioning that the timing of Easter was based on the moon too but I knew that Easter wasn't quite as mobile as Ramadan.

We went to visit my parents for Christmas as usual. I wanted to show that we were still very much part of the family and could participate in important family occasions – even in Ramadan. My mother thoughtfully adapted the usual routine. The lights were left on at night so that Julian and I could creep downstairs to have an early breakfast; she even bought dates – and fig biscuits – for us to break our fast. Everyone gathered for the Christmas lunch at four o'clock instead of three hours earlier.

My father was not happy about having to wait so long for his food: he developed severe migraines if he did not eat substantial and regular meals. Safiyya, emotionally tuned in to the atmosphere around her, spent most of the 'lunchtime' screaming. Then we had to fit in a quick birthday celebration for my sister that same afternoon. The calm Ramadan spirit of self-restraint was missing – and it looked like we were definitely dampening the festive spirit of Christmas. My father suggested we either move Ramadan or stay at home for the following Christmas.

Choosing our celebration

We did stay at home the following year. For the first time in my life, I didn't have Christmas with my parents and instead broke fast in the afternoon with one of Julian's Muslim aunts. It was probably the best decision for us all although my mother was disappointed that she wouldn't be able to take her first ever grandchild to Santa's grotto. But this break with tradition finally forced me to choose what was more important to me. Was it Ramadan? Or was it Christmas? My father helped me to make that choice.

Julian and I decided we would now get each other presents at *Eid* rather than Christmas – and decorate our house then too. We felt we deserved to celebrate after completing an entire month of fasting. But we also thought we needed to be clearer about our own identity if we stood a chance of helping our little girl with hers. We were still very comfortable with visiting my parents at Christmas, affirming family ties and giving everyone presents but finally established that Christmas wasn't our celebration.

Christmas cheer

At school, nursery and all around us, Christmas continued to dominate the month of December – as well as the months before it.

The children were all involved in organized Christmas activities. At playgroup, Asim was a shepherd. Amaani was an angel: she looked sweet and innocent dressed up in ballet shoes, fairy wings and a plastic halo. As a Muslim, I believed in angels: they were spiritual genderless beings, part of the unseen world, who throughout time had appeared in male human form to different Prophets – including Abraham, Lot and Muhammad – as well as to Mary. I knew they didn't look anything like Amaani.

Safiyya's Nativity Play seemed to be progressing well. A few Muslim parents had withdrawn their children completely, as the Qur'an never mentioned the 'no room at the inn' story. But most Muslim children took part, with low-profile roles: they were the sheep and the Wise Men. No Muslim boy was playing the part of Joseph – for Muslims, his relationship with Mary was unclear but he definitely wasn't the father of Jesus. And no Muslim girl was playing the part of Mary: Mary was highly revered in Islam, being the mother of a special Prophet. But where was Safiyya? I waited and waited. She had gone backstage wearing a black t-shirt and trousers and I hadn't seen her since.

Safiyya appeared in the final five minutes of the play, in the choir. She launched with gusto into a song entitled 'Jesus, Son of God'. I couldn't help being disappointed. I had spoken with Safiyya about the Muslim belief in the story: that Angel Gabriel had appeared to Mary and that the birth of Jesus was a miracle. I had asked her to imagine the additional miracle of baby Jesus speaking in his cradle, mentioned in the Qur'an (19:29–33). But I had also explained to Safiyya that although ultimately we were all God's children, Jesus was Mary's son. Now she was singing with all her heart that Jesus was God's son. My mother used to say to us: 'I feel like I am talking to a brick wall.' I was feeling like that too.

'Did you enjoy the play?' asked her teacher expectantly, as I went to pick Safiyya up after the performance. 'I can see that the children have put much work into this. It must have taken you hours,' I said, genuinely appreciative. But I then tried to be as gentle as I could: 'Next time though, it might be better if the Muslim children didn't have to sing about Jesus being the Son of God.' I assumed the teacher hadn't realized that the words directly contradicted aspects of the faith of some of her pupils; she possibly had even tried to be 'culturally sensitive' by casting Safiyya in the choir rather than in the main story. Now she looked deflated.

Like Christians, Muslims loved the story of Jesus' birth. I thought I was perhaps part of a minority among the audience for genuinely believing in it. And so it was unfortunate for us all that our differences in faith were being emphasized rather than our similarities. I went away deflated too.

Selective visiting

The children saw a lot of Father Christmas. He visited Tumble Tots and Bethany Babes playgroup and nursery; he even came to school. Everywhere he went, he gave the children presents. He was clearly a very busy man, whoever he was.

Just before Christmas, I took all the children to visit Great-Great-Uncle Roland at his nursing home. There were two huge Christmas trees in the lobby area; 'Away in a Manger' was playing in the background. Uncle Roland and his two elderly friends looked delighted to see three little people. They showed the children the trees and the lights and they elaborated on the details of Father

Christmas's toy factory, the reindeer and the difficulty of squeezing down a chimney. Safiyya listened politely. Amaani hadn't yet learnt to speak properly. Then there was Asim. Asim kept piping up: 'But I'm Muslim'. But none of the senior citizens took notice of Asim's interruptions: his speech wasn't that clear, they were all hard of hearing and they probably hadn't met too many Muslims before.

When we got in the car, Asim spelt out his confusion: 'Why do these really old grown-ups believe in Father Christmas when we know he isn't real?' I tried to explain. 'Well they don't think he's real but they think you think he is.' Life was seriously complicated.

Father Christmas never came down the chimney to my children. When the family gathered once again at my parents' house, he managed to visit my niece and nephew in the room where they were sleeping but never appeared in our children's room. Asim thought this made perfect sense because for him there was a straightforward link between belief in Father Christmas and belief in Jesus' divine qualities. 'You see, he knows we are Muslim and that Jasper and Katrina are Christian,' he observed. For someone who wasn't real, Father Christmas was very clever.

Two days after Christmas, the lady at the checkout till at Sainsbury's supermarket asked Asim what Father Christmas had brought him. 'Nothing' he answered, simply. The woman looked at me in horror. I felt she wanted to ask me: 'What kind of mean mother are you?' But I didn't expect to have to justify my parenting style to the shop's staff. I had only come in to buy some bread and toilet rolls.

Hungry babies

Ramadan kept coming. 'Does your toddler have to fast?' asked my interested American colleague Karl. I was a bit shocked that he even needed to ask. But the whole religion of Islam was rather a mystery to him – Karl had also asked me whether my baby had to wear a scarf. Other people came up to me separately with the same question on fasting. For them, Islam was clearly so extreme that it could easily require my young child not to eat or drink for 12 hours a day for one month a year.

The only aspect of Ramadan that my workmates could see was my lack of eating and drinking. They couldn't see that it was simply a means to a variety of ends. I thought about God so much more than usual, even when I did the most mundane of tasks. I thought about God as I brushed my teeth because I had to be careful not to swallow any water. I thought about God as I cut up vegetables, avoiding my usual habit of popping a piece of raw carrot into my mouth as I chopped. I thought twice before screaming at Asim and Amaani for throwing Rice Krispies all over the floor – Muhammad had said God didn't need the fast of one who was angry.[7] And I developed patience as I waited until sunset before enjoying a cup of tea. How could a child gain any of those benefits? Amaani was still working on learning how to talk – and she didn't drink tea.

I explained to Karl that there was no obligation for a child to fast until he or she reached puberty. 'That makes a bit more sense,' he commented. If Karl had seen me with Amaani, I don't think he would have worried. Amaani fasted in hour-long instalments: she ate three meals a day, with snacks in between. When it was time for me to break my fast, she tested my developing patience to the limit: she clambered on to my lap and wanted to help herself to my food too.

A sense of community

The children's routine continued. Safiyya was having weekly ballet lessons, which ended at 4.30pm. Sunset in November was at 4.35pm. I knew I had to rush to break my fast and quickly weighed up my options: I hadn't had time to prepare anything at home; the mosque was marginally closer to the ballet school and I knew that – unlike at home – food at the mosque would probably be ready and waiting, brought there by rather more organized members of the community.

I went to the mosque and made my way to the community hall. Safiyya was still in her tutu, one younger sibling was hanging on to my legs and the youngest was in my arms. There were no women in the mosque, but there were lots of men. I arrived just a few minutes after everyone else had broken fast. The mosque elders rushed to set us up with a tiny table near the men's long trellis one. And then three bearded men hovered to ensure I had everything I would need for both myself and the children. I was touched by their flexibility and generosity – particularly as they had been fasting too.

I knew many people would come back to the mosque later in the evening, to perform the additional *tarawih* prayers – it was always preferable to pray in congregation if possible. But I stayed at home with my children so that the other men and women would be able to focus in peace. Asim climbed on my back every time I went to prostrate on the floor; Amaani clutched like a limpet on to my front. It was hard to think abstractly about God and the signs of His creation when one of His little miracles was experimenting with holding on to my shoulders using only his hands and another was busy examining my eyelids. I resolved that next time I would put the children to bed well before I prayed the extra prayers.

The Night of Power

Extra prayers could be offered every night in Ramadan, but there was one night during which it was considered even better to pray than all the others. That night was called the Night of Power.[8]

The Night of Power falls within the last 10 days of Ramadan, with the date traditionally set for the twenty-seventh night. It was referred to in the Qur'an as being 'better than a thousand months' (97:3). As a Muslim, I believe that it was originally the night when the Qur'an was first revealed to Muhammad; now it is the night every year when angels descend to earth. It is the night to spend hours in contemplation, prayer, and reading the Qur'an – if possible right through until the rising of the dawn, known in Arabic as al-Fajr.

Except, in that November in 2004, the Night of Power was the night when the Americans launched an operation in Fallujah – a city referred to in Iraq as 'the city of mosques'. It was an operation known as 'Phantom Fury' in English and *al-Fajr* in Arabic.[9] More than half of Fallujah's 50,000 houses were destroyed; thousands were killed. It would have been devastating on any night of the year but I knew – as I knew millions of other Muslims would – that it was the twenty-seventh night of Ramadan, that most special night known as the Night of Power. It was like obliterating the English city of Canterbury on Easter Sunday. It felt like an insult that the rest of the world would not notice.[10] Perhaps it was just a tragic coincidence.

Counting up

I kept my children's attention focused on events closer to home.

They were busy checking on their Ramadan calendars. The supermarket Asda was stocking some that were filled with chocolate. As a child, I used to love my own chocolate-filled calendars for Christmas but I felt that this didn't fit very well with the ethos of self-restraint in Ramadan. So, although craft had never been my strong point, the children and I had made our own chocolate-free ones.

Asim and Safiyya had decorated their calendars prolifically and without any sense of self-restraint: they were now covered in fluffy balls and coloured sticks and bits of crepe paper. Underneath the numbered Post-it note relating to the relevant day, the children discovered the good deeds they had to do, which ranged from singing a song about Ramadan to giving Mummy a hug and from saying a quick prayer to sweeping the kitchen floor. They excelled at hugging and failed miserably at sweeping. But the thought was there: they were trying their best to do good deeds and they were fasting from the bad.

With the excitement building up, they counted the days until *Eid*. There was one logistical issue: if the new moon marking the start of the next lunar month was sighted before the dawn of the thirtieth fast, then Ramadan would be over after only 29 days; there would be no Day Thirty. Advent calendars never had that problem. I tried to explain it to the children.

Confusing children

Asim now thought he knew all about Ramadan and decided to enlighten his nursery teacher when I collected him at going-home time. 'You see, it's when you get to drink lemonade,' he explained. His teacher looked at me quizzically: I had no idea what Asim was talking about. The following day his teacher saw him drinking juice, and asked him: 'Is that part of Ramadan too?' Asim then remembered: 'Oh yes, we have lemonade at *Eid*, not Ramadan. Ramadan is when we fast.' And then he added: 'I'm fasting now.'

Asim had got confused. I only allowed my children to have fizzy drinks at parties and had told them that *Eid* was the biggest lemonade-drinking party of them all. But I couldn't account for why he thought he was fasting while he was drinking. Two weeks later, Asim had worked it all out: 'When you fast, you don't eat or drink and you be nice,' he pronounced confidently to his little sister Amaani, as if he had known for years.

Asim's friend Nabihah also successfully confused the people around her. Her neighbour had offered to take her to the park, along with her own little girl. Nabihah's mother Rahat happily sent her off for a play-date, but was surprised that her daughter appeared back home within half an hour. The neighbour explained that she had been concerned about Nabihah. As soon as they had reached the playground, she had offered the children some snacks but Nabihah had refused. 'I can't,' she had replied, 'I'm fasting'. The neighbour was trying her best to understand. 'Is she not even allowed a sip of water?' she asked Rahat. Rahat couldn't believe what she was hearing: Nabihah had last eaten just five minutes before the neighbour had popped by to collect her; Nabihah wasn't fasting.

Eid at school

After all the children's Ramadan experiences of fasting – or, in some cases, imaginary fasting – they were looking forward to the festival of *Eid*.

I had thought the teachers at Safiyya's school were not even aware it was *Eid*. But shortly before *Eid*, Safiyya came home with two new whiteboard markers in her possession. I was curious. Her answer was elaborate. 'The school held an *Eid* assembly. Then we all sang *Eid* songs – and I stood in front of everyone to lead them, as not many people knew the words. Then we all played *Eid* party games. I won "Pass the Parcel". And the pens are my *Eid* prize,' she said triumphantly. I was overwhelmed by the effort the school was making.

The following day, it was parents' evening. After discussing Safiyya's performance in spelling and times tables, I thanked the teacher for helping to make *Eid* such a special part of the Muslim children's experience in school. She looked at me blankly. 'But we didn't do anything,' she said. She was also missing two whiteboard markers. The following morning, I told Safiyya that I had found out the truth: she had stolen classroom equipment. I marched the subdued little girl in to the classroom, made her apologize to the teacher and watched her hand back her special '*Eid* prize'.

Eid in Iran

I wrote a letter to the Head of the school, requesting permission to take the children away for a week to celebrate *Eid* with their grandparents who were now expatriates in Tehran, Iran. The Head wrote back promptly, saying: 'I agree it would be a unique cultural opportunity, and I wish you all the best for your trip.'

I started packing. I made sure we took the child car seats, although the moment we were met at Tehran airport, I could see the seats would be unusable: Iranian cars didn't have seatbelts. The roads were both chaotic and lethal. While I was there, the Iranian media reported that 15,000 deaths had occurred on the roads over the previous 12 months: it was not a reassuring statistic. We drove – in any direction – around roundabouts that were crowded with refugees looking for work: Julian's mother explained that Iran was one of the most welcoming countries in the world, sheltering around two million Afghan refugees.

The children loved visiting their grandparents. I loved visiting them too. I also enjoyed experiencing the architecture of the ancient mosques, the relaxed atmosphere of the parks – where boys and girls were getting to know each other, usually supervised by their family – and the tearooms.

I had brought long and rather dark skirts to wear since I had seen photographs in English newspapers of Iranian women and so I knew they were always dressed in black. But I was overdressed: most women were in jeans, and many were heavily made-up, wearing their scarves as far back on their heads as they could get away with, revealing their heavily coiffed hair. Whenever I went out, I just had to make sure I was wearing a long top that covered down to my thighs – the top could be of any material, colour or style. There were indeed women all in black, keeping their cloaks wrapped around them with one arm, but they seemed to constitute a minority among the fashion scene that was Tehran.

The last couple of days of Ramadan were quiet. Julian's stepfather, who held a senior position in his company, mentioned that the only person in the office who broke fast with him was the tea boy. That was strange: his office was staffed entirely by Muslims. The festival of *Eid* itself seemed to be a non-event in Tehran – the streets around us were quiet, and I could not find *Eid* even being mentioned in the English-speaking Iranian newspapers. I must have been looking in the wrong place. We went to the ski-slopes outside Tehran, and watched both Iranian men and women experiment with their skiing techniques, in their own way celebrating *Eid*.

Eid back home

Now that I knew a lot of people in my community, I found it was much more fun to celebrate *Eid* in my own way, in my own country.

The day before *Eid*, children each brought in an *Eid* gift for their teacher and handed out sweets to the other children in the class. Two school-friends – one Muslim and one non-Muslim – came to the house to help stick paper-chains together and decorate the children's bedrooms. I had imagined this would contribute towards creating a festive spirit: I hadn't anticipated that I would then spend much of the afternoon breaking up squabbles about which colour paper-chain belonged to whom, in between frantically cooking and baking to be ready for *Eid*.

I took the children out of school for the day of *Eid* itself, despite the clear disapproval of the school receptionist – who felt it was very unfair that my children were also going to have time off for Christmas – and of my father, who felt we should be observing the holidays only of the country in which we were living. I helped the children to dress up: Safiyya wore an Indian-style top with flowing skirt and matching Indian scarf; Asim sported a pure white Arab *thobe*, which happened to reveal his Spiderman vest underneath; and Amaani was looking demure in an English dress. And then the phone rang: it was my mother. 'What would you like for Christmas, Lucy?' my mother asked. 'I can't really think about it right now. It's a bit busy here,' I told her. But I promised to call her back.

We drove fast to the mosque and the sermon began. It was in Urdu, and I didn't understand a word of it. Neither did Julian – and neither did my children. I wished that more *imams* in England would adapt to the needs of their predominantly English-speaking congregation and speak English. It would make us feel at home.

Julian, the children and I came back to our house and the children unwrapped their presents. As parents, we were able to take all the credit as no one had come down the chimney bearing gifts. And then our house began to fill up with Muslim friends and family – all bringing contributions of food; some bringing small presents. Lena, Rachel and Claire converged on the house, along with their husbands and children. Arab friends came too and so did other British Muslim friends – including Nasheeba and Saji.

Once school had finished for the day, neighbours dropped by too. 'Happy Diwali,' said my neighbour Jane, as she knocked on the door. It had become a joke between us: both Diwali and *Eid* were such 'foreign' celebrations that many people didn't know the difference between them. 'Happy Diwali' I replied. Her children tucked into the gingerbread boys and girls with great enthusiasm. My school-run partner Susie – as keen to help as always – bustled around making tea for everyone. Late into the evening, the children fell into bed exhausted.

I was exhausted too: once everyone else had left, I found it a struggle even to climb the stairs to go to bed. But I went to sleep happy, happy to be part of such a vibrant and diverse community. I hoped that my children were taking it all in.

9 The Next Generation

> 'O our Sustainer! Grant that our spouses and our offspring be a joy to our eyes, and cause us to be foremost among those who are conscious of You!'
>
> (Qur'an 25:74)

> 'No gift among all the gifts of a father to his child is better than education.'[1]
>
> (Saying of Muhammad)

Once my children began to interact with adults and other children, their Arabic names began to cause a little confusion.

What's in a name?

Safiyya obligingly responded to Sophie, Saffira, Sapphire and Sophia. 'As in Loren?' asked the dentist. Safiyya wasn't sure. When I took Asim to the shoe shop, the assistant asked him to repeat his name three times. Eventually she asked: 'Can I call you Fred?' And then there was Amaani. A father of a child at Amaani's nursery asked her: 'Are you a victim of Harry Potter fever?' Amaani didn't know what he was talking about; I didn't either until I realized he must have thought he had heard me calling her Hermione. A mother at playgroup commented: 'That's a very exclusive name – I just love his bags.' I had to tell her Giorgio Armani had absolutely nothing to do with it. Even Asim

found these Arabic names complicated: he thought his friend Isa –
which was Arabic for Jesus – was called Easter.

But I soon discovered it wasn't only Muslim children's names that
could be misunderstood. Asim came home and told me his new best
friend was a girl called Medicine. I suggested she wasn't. And he was
adamant that Medicine was her name. I checked the pre-school class
list – she was called Madison.

Pork pies

Safiyya was going to the local state school. I had filled in numerous
forms before school started: contact details, the home-school
agreement, allergies, even a sun-cream permission form. Safiyya
had to fill in a form herself, although hers mainly involved drawing a
picture of herself and writing her name. I had also filled in a diet form:
clearly stating that Safiyya didn't eat pork.

Safiyya knew she was not meant to eat pork. When I had been
teaching her the letters of the alphabet in the summer before school
started, we made a series of three-letter words using magnetic fridge
letters. But Safiyya refused to let me compile the word 'ham'. She told
me firmly: 'We eat lamb not ham'; she took away the letter 'h' from
the fridge and rewrote the word with an 'l'. Fundamentalists start
young these days – even if they can't spell.

As a child and teenager, I used to love the taste of bacon, and the
crackling on roast pork, although I was never a fan of that traditional
northern English recipe for black pudding made from pig's blood.
Over 10 years had now passed since I had eaten any pork.

There were a number of medical reasons why I wasn't allowed to
eat pork: as a student I had listened carefully to the teachings of a
well-known Muslim Professor called Jamal Badawi on this subject.[2] I
knew pigs ate anything, including household and commercial
waste – a factory in the south-east that I had toured around as a
student sent their remnants to feed the local pigs. I knew pigs also

carried various types of worms although I presumed these were less likely to be a problem in England, where strict hygiene rules were enforced. I knew pig meat was high in cholesterol and very fatty: a Catholic member of Julian's extended family had been told by the doctor to avoid it for those reasons. And I also knew that the Muslims weren't alone in avoiding pork – Jews didn't eat it either and neither did Jesus.[3] But the overriding reason that I didn't eat pork was that I believed that, through the Qur'an, God had asked me not to (5:3). And so I had to bring up the children not to eat it as well.

Yet, for the first term at school, Safiyya ate pork – lots of it. I only found out due to my Malaysian friend Saji, who was a teaching assistant at Safiyya's school. As part of Saji's school duties, she supervised the lunchtime chaos. Towards the end of term, she noticed Safiyya eating gammon. Saji told me she immediately went to the dinner ladies and explained to them: 'This child is Muslim; she doesn't eat pork.' 'That child has been eating bacon, sausages and ham all term,' they replied. 'She's not Muslim, she's white.' The following morning, I handed a photograph of Safiyya to the head dinner lady, along with a note specifying that she didn't eat every type of pork-containing product I could think of. It worked – although I detected Safiyya seemed disappointed.

Safiyya's fixation with pigs continued. In her class assembly, each child had to dress up as an animal. When I saw Safiyya on stage, I discovered she had chosen to be a pig. All the other Muslim children were being sheep and cows. The Muslim mother watching the assembly next to me commented, with a pitying smile: 'Your daughter is dressed as a pig.' As if I hadn't noticed. I knew it didn't really matter though: all animals are God's creatures. Pigs are pretty smart too. And they are pink.

By contrast, Asim was obsessed about not eating pork. When a friend whom I had got to know through Safiyya's school kindly bought him a packet of Polo Mints, he refused to eat any until he had checked with her that there was no pork inside. My father had always taught us: 'Never assume anything.' Asim was taking this advice to extremes.

A two-way exchange

In the second term, the school distributed their three-year development plan. Ofsted, the official body for inspecting schools, had described the school as excellent, with just one priority area for improvement – pupils' 'spiritual, moral and cultural development'. I knew that approximately one in ten of the pupils was Muslim. When the school invited comments from parents, I couldn't resist.

My friend Nasheeba's children were at the school too and so Nasheeba and I worked together to compile a list of practical suggestions. We requested that the school should know when the Islamic holidays were rather than individual parents having to inform the teachers and we asked for an assembly on *Eid* and an internal 'postbox' for those children who were making *Eid* cards. And we suggested that Muslims could contribute, both in delivering occasional value-based assemblies and in providing training for teachers on Islam, if the staff felt it would be beneficial. Many parents signed the letter to show their support.

Nasheeba and I were soon summoned to see the Headmistress. The prospect was scary. But once we were in the office the atmosphere was cordial. The Head's main priority was to get the Urdu-speaking mothers to speak English so that they could be involved both in their child's homework and in the life of the school; she wondered if we could help. This language barrier was a real issue, relating to all mothers whose home language wasn't English. Nasheeba was bilingual and offered her services. I couldn't help: I only spoke English.

But the language issue wasn't a Muslim one and also didn't relate directly to the children. We wanted to make sure the Muslim children felt that their identity was accepted both at home and at school, like everyone else's. The Head made a few changes. A calendar detailing all religious holidays was put up in the staff room. I never saw a postbox, or any sign of a Muslim being involved in the regular assemblies, but the Head made space in the agenda of a teachers' weekly meeting for a 30-minute training session on Islam. I led this session with the South African *imam* from the mosque – the Head told me afterwards that she had learned that Muslims believe in the same Prophets as her.

The following year, Safiyya's year group was actively involved in an assembly on *Eid*, supervised by the religious education coordinator, who happened to be Hindu. At school, Safiyya never played *Eid* 'Pass the Parcel' but she did finally get to sing a song about *Eid*.

Easter service

At Easter-time, the local Bethany Babes playgroup attended a short service in the church. I went along with Asim and Amaani. Asim explained it all to me afterwards. 'They killed Jesus,' he declared. I asked him who did. 'The children did', he replied. I think he had got confused about the children who had greeted Jesus with branches of palm trees when he had originally arrived in Jerusalem. 'And who is Jesus?' I asked him. 'Jesus is,' replied Asim, with no further elaboration. 'And where does he live?' 'He lives at home with his mummy, of course.' Of course.

Safiyya also attended an Easter service at the church, along with the rest of her primary school and the parents. The children, all aged between four and ten, sat cross-legged in rows on the church floor. I noticed many of the school pupils could not take their eyes off the crown that had been made of thorns and the large cross propped up next to the vicar. The vicar explained the Easter story to the young children. It then occurred to me that this was quite confusing for those young children who didn't hear much about Christianity on a regular basis. In December, they had learned Jesus was a baby and had a special birth; now, just a few months later, they were learning that he was an adult and had a special death.

At the end of his short sermon, the vicar gave the children an ultimatum. 'You need to decide: either I am mad, or Jesus Christ our Lord died on the Cross to save us all.' Did it have to be so clear cut? I had known the vicar for over five years – I was sure he wasn't mad. I was also not convinced that Jesus Christ had died on the cross to save me. Where did that leave me? And more importantly, where did that leave the children?

I spoke to Asim and Safiyya about the Muslim view of the Easter story. 'Muslims don't believe Jesus saved us. If you believe in God and are good, we believe God will reward you and you will find in Paradise whatever you like. And Muslims don't think that Jesus died on the cross, even though it looked like it.[4] He was special – he went to Heaven alive. One day, he will come back to Earth and rule over us all with kindness and fairness.' I waited for them to process what I had just said.

Asim told me thoughtfully: 'I want to be a fish in Paradise': he had seen *Finding Nemo* and thought being a fish looked quite fun. Safiyya said sincerely: 'When Jesus comes back, I really want to invite him home for tea.' 'Oh so do I,' agreed her little brother, presumably hoping for a play-date.

A local Muslim friend of mine Sofia should have been involved in celebrating Easter at her own children's primary school. Her five-year-old son Danyal, named after a prophet, was featuring in an Easter Bonnet parade. But Sofia had just given birth to her third child. Life was busy – and Sofia forgot about the parade. She sent him to school without his hat. In the parade, Danyal looked different to all the other children. When Sofia came to collect him, Danyal's teacher came up to her. 'We noticed he didn't wear his hat. We were wondering if it was against your religion.' Sofia had to apologize and explain: she had just forgotten; she was very happy for him to wear his hat, and she was also very happy for him to learn about Easter.

Celebrating everything

As part of the British curriculum, the children were learning about many different faiths. Safiyya learnt about Judaism. She came home telling me all about it. 'Jewish people speak like this, Mummy', she told me eagerly: she then put on her 'poshest' voice and said 'Oh, hello.' And then in her normal voice, added: 'I know they speak like that, I heard it.' I asked Safiyya if the Jewish people said anything else. 'Oh no, just hello,' she replied. It must have been a very short extract they were listening to. Or else she had a very short memory.

And then there was Islam. Safiyya learnt that all Qur'ans must be wrapped in a green cloth. Safiyya was now convinced we were not proper Muslims: the Qur'ans we had at home were not wrapped in anything. We always kept the Qur'an on the highest shelf, and made sure no other books were stacked on top of it, and we did keep it clean. But we didn't wrap it in a cloth of any colour. She didn't mention anything about what was inside the book, which for me was rather more important.

All the children loved Hinduism: the elaborate tales, the vivid images, and the Festival of Lights. My school-run partner Susie and I decided to complement the school curriculum by taking all of our children along to the town centre after school to see the vibrant Diwali celebrations. People were dressed up, dancing, holding lanterns and banging drums, forming a long and joyful procession around the streets.

I explained to Safiyya that Hindus were celebrating Diwali. I was instantly corrected. 'No, Mummy. Everybody celebrates everything, my teacher says so'. I think she was right – there were lots of English-looking people participating alongside the local Indian Hindu community. Safiyya then proceeded to tell me she wanted to be Hindu. I felt she was a little young to be making such a momentous decision but I didn't want her to feel restricted in her choices. And so I told her: 'That's fine, you can choose what you are – but you do need to know that Hindus don't eat beef.' She stopped wanting to be Hindu.

Safiyya had already been told directly by a few other Muslim children that she wasn't Muslim. 'You are not brown and you don't speak Urdu,' they explained. 'But I am a bit brown,' she said to me, as she related this story through her tears. She was referring to her hair colour. I reassured her that it didn't matter what colour she was. I also reminded her that I was incapable of speaking Urdu too and that I was sure God would understand our English.

British and Muslim

I was asked by a teacher at a local girls' private school to talk to a hundred non-Muslim seventeen-year-olds about Islam and Britishness. I asked Allia to come with me, dressed in her customary black: I thought it would be good for the pupils to recognize the diversity within Islam both in culture and practice. Allia spoke to the pupils about Islam, explaining the tenets of the faith and the history of Islam in Britain. And then I spoke about being Muslim and being British.

I asked the children to get involved: I asked them to think about different lifestyle practices. If they had to tell their parents that they were going to take part in a particular activity, would their parents mind? Or would their parents go mad – or think their child was? The sixth-formers had four things to decide. Which customs were acceptable to both Muslims and the majority British community? Which were unique in terms of acceptability to Muslims? Which were unique to everyone else? And which were acceptable to neither?

The pupils surprised me with their lateral thinking. Before long, the two overlapping circles I had drawn on the overhead projector were filled up, as pupils came and wrote down their thoughts. In the 'Muslim only' section, the girls had written habits that their parents would think were slightly strange if the children wanted to participate in them: five daily prayers, Arabic, Ramadan, *Hajj*, *Eid*, and the scarf. In the 'majority British only' segment, they had noted down practices which their parents wouldn't mind if they got involved in, but where they thought a Muslim parent might 'flip': alcohol, living together, Easter, pubs and clubs.

The overlapping section of the circle was the busiest. Words written down included: weddings, community, charity, places of worship, holidays, sports, work and fashion. The pupils knew that people did not all do those things in exactly the same way but believed each of those activities was important both to Muslims and to everyone else. Finally, outside the circle, were attitudes that everybody felt were – or should be – unacceptable to everyone: racism, honour killings, illegal drugs and forced marriage.

They examined the piece of work and could think of nothing more to add.

Teaching the teachers

Six months later, I was asked by a school governor at a local primary school to talk to the teachers about issues directly affecting their Muslim pupils. Once again, I asked Allia to help. The school had many issues: parents were not involved in the life of the school; some of the girls wanted to wear their scarves for sports lessons; and pupils were being taken out of school by their parents to visit relatives primarily in Pakistan for extended periods of time.

Allia and I prepared a teacher quiz to test their knowledge, a word association game, and a series of slides highlighting the research on what made a successful school with minority ethnic pupils.[5] The next section covered how the British Muslim culture was changing, from an immigrant culture to a culture of belonging, where a key issue for all was the upbringing and education of the next generation.[6] The presentation moved on to explain the Muslim belief and the Muslim values of community, parenting, education and modesty. It briefly mentioned the Islamic value of punctuality – and explained that Muslims in England hadn't fully embraced that one yet.

And then the presentation examined practical considerations affecting pupils.[7] There were some religious needs of the pupils, mainly centring on diet, special festivals, dress, hair covering and fasting. These children were still young – while Islam didn't require them to wear long clothes, cover their hair, or fast, some wanted to and some had parents who wanted them to. We also included some practical ways that might make all pupils feel valued – through obtaining music from the cultures and faiths of all the pupils, through involving the pupils appropriately during annual events such as Christmas and Mothers Day and through positive community activities such as sponsoring an orphan.

Islam was a sensitive subject and I had been warned by the Governor that we would be presenting to a sensitive audience who were very aware that Muslims made up the majority of their secular state school. I emailed the presentation to a senior Ofsted inspector to check it for accuracy: he described it as 'thorough, comprehensive and clear.' Allia and I both prayed that whatever would happen would be for the best. Finally, after making arrangements for childcare, we were ready to go.

Taking offence

The session was a nightmare. We offended everybody. We offended Muslims when we said it would have been Islamically acceptable for the pupils to have said the word 'sausages' when the school photographer came, instead of staying silent – and when we said that the school did not have to ban the film *Babe,* featuring an animated pig. I specifically offended a Muslim woman wearing short sleeves when I explained the Islamic dress code: she told me: 'Go and live in the real world.' And we offended everybody else when we presented the slide that the girls in the private school had developed. The staff interpreted the diagram as saying that Allia and I thought all Muslim values were positive and all British values were negative –

and that we were also implying no Muslim ever drank alcohol or went to clubs. They all started shouting out at once. Due to the chaos, I unhelpfully forgot to tell them from where it had originated. And the atmosphere was too hostile to establish any group discussion about practical ways to help the children.

Allia left to get her preschool children who were being looked after by in-laws. I left to pick up Asim who had been with my friend Rahat and had a strong cup of tea at her house. I felt like I had been wrung out to dry.

A week later I got some feedback. My training credentials were being questioned in meetings both among staff members and in governing body meetings by the Chair of Governors – even though I had now highlighted the contribution of the teenage girls. Interestingly, some of the Muslim teaching assistants had now started to read the Bible. I telephoned my father to let him know what was happening in my life and he told me he was right by my side, ready to sue. Whom he was going to sue, and for what, I am not sure, but for me his support was reassuring. I lost four kilos.

After two long months, the governors and teachers stopped questioning the training. No one sued. I put back the four kilos. A sad outcome for me was that that the schoolchildren had not benefited in any way. The headteacher left due to unspecified 'stress' and a new head came in – one who had been featured on the BBC children's programme *Newsround* for her approach in making all children in her school feel valued. She was ready to nurture the children to their full potential, whatever faith they had. The next generation was being looked after.

I started paying some attention to my own family.

Learning backwards

Safiyya had been reading English for two years: I thought it was time she learnt to read Arabic. I was looking forward to the blissful time together that I had imagined. We spent a month going through the letters of the alphabet, with the help of an Arabic jigsaw puzzle from a Saudi Arabian branch of the Early Learning Centre. Then I took her to a quiet room upstairs for 15 minutes each day to teach her how to join the letters up and how to read a few words and phrases at a time – all 'backwards', from right to left.

But the sessions were not blissful. Safiyya was kicking and screaming upstairs with me as she resented being stretched in this way. Asim and Amaani were crying and screaming downstairs because they wanted to be with us. After four months of tantrums, I felt Safiyya was ready to read the Qur'an. And I felt exhausted.

Most of the Muslim children in Safiyya's school were learning to read Qur'an through the after-school *madrasa*, where they went for two hours every day. Safiyya's schoolteacher told me that this left little time for the pupils to do their homework, to become involved in other after-school activities or meet up with school friends. I wanted Safiyya to do all those things but I wanted her to learn about her faith with her Muslim peers too.

I went along to see if I could picture my children learning in the *madrasa* environment. There were more than 300 children learning in two halls – noise levels were high. The majority of the time was spent reciting Qur'an in Arabic in small groups, although they did have textbooks for other subjects, such as Islamic character – focusing on positive values such as honesty and abstaining from negative ones such as arrogance – and *fiqh*, understanding Islamic law, particularly concerning rituals related to cleanliness, prayer, and fasting.

To me, there seemed to be little opportunity to inculcate a faith in God – and a deep love of God – that would carry the children through life's trials and tribulations. And there seemed little opportunity to appreciate the signs of His creation. The learning style was based predominantly on repetition and rote learning, rather than including the techniques used at school, such as discussion, group work, and hands-on experience. These children's 'Muslim life' was very different to their school life.

Getting started

And so Nasheeba and I decided to start our own *madrasa*. We couldn't call it a *madrasa* though – that term conjured up too many negative connotations in both of our minds. So we called it a 'Muslim after-school club.' We gave it the name 'Fitra', an acronym for 'Fun, Islamic Teaching, Reading and Activities.' 'Fitra' was also Arabic for the innate God-consciousness and childhood innocence with which Muslims believe every child is born. The *madrasa* name seemed appropriate.

Fitra had a bumpy start. We persuaded various mothers to come weekly with their children to a local community centre, which was very welcoming and charged us a discounted rate. The NCT playgroup kindly shared its chairs and toys with us free of charge. But although we managed to cover the rent, we had no money left over to invest in Islamic books, workbooks and posters. I applied for funding, detailing Fitra's extensive racial diversity, which included British children from a variety of origins, including white English, Pakistani, Indian, Malay, Egyptian, Iraqi, Sudanese and Syrian. But everywhere I applied, the *madrasa* was turned down. The one grant Fitra was awarded was allocated directly to the community centre, for it to choose and keep equipment – and they had not even applied for the grant. I turned that grant down myself.

We moved rent-free to the mosque, which generously donated money for equipment, including toys for the under-fives.

Dog in the mosque

As summer was approaching, we were invited to take part in a joint performance with the main *madrasa*, held in the mosque for the benefit of all the parents. Fitra parents and children alike were enthusiastic. My age group, the three-to-five year olds, dressed up as things that they believed God had made. When it was their turn to perform, they took it in turns to stand up in front of all the parents. 'Allah made the sun', 'Allah made the moon', 'Allah made the cat', they said, in their shy but sweet voices.

Each child was greeted with applause – until the three-year-old child with a dog mask appeared on stage. The majority of the audience started talking avidly in Urdu. The mother suddenly hauled her child away. The remaining children started to sing but there was too much commotion to hear the words. The youngest group was then forcibly stopped. I found out the problem: the community thought the sun was acceptable; the moon was acceptable; even the cat was acceptable ... but dogs should not be in the mosque.[8] My teaching credentials were being openly questioned again albeit by a totally different audience.

The older groups took over: they started reciting Arabic verses of the Qur'an. And the audience started warming up. I went home confused by the incident. I knew the *hadith* that utensils had to be washed if a dog had touched them – but there was no dog in the mosque: it was a three-year-old boy.

My friend Zahra telephoned me that evening. 'It's going to be OK,' she said, 'I told them that the child was not a dog; he was a cow.'

Joining the club

Fortunately, over summer, the incident seemed to be forgotten. The *madrasa* was welcomed back into the mosque for the following term. More children joined us and we needed more space. My age group was thoughtfully allowed to use a private room in the *imam's* house. I was glad: I didn't want everyone to hear our attempts at singing.

Nasheeba moved away to London and I started working on the *madrasa* with two other friends: Rahat, the friend who had looked after Asim while I had been attempting to train the teachers, and another, Farah, an ex-City lawyer. Both had spent many of their childhood years in Pakistan and both shared Fitra's vision. Rahat had useful connections with the local Arab community. The Arab ladies added to the credibility of the *madrasa* among the Muslims, were able to improve the children's Qur'an pronunciation, and also knew many more children who wanted to join.

But we had a problem. On a cold and wet Tuesday in November, the mosque's Head of Education paid us a visit. He told us that 'our children' were disrupting the learning of 'their' children as our classes ran immediately before the main *madrasa* started – and the children who arrived slightly early for the larger *madrasa* had to wait for those few minutes. He said that a group of 'their' older children were learning in a concrete-floored hall while 'our' children had been given a private room with a carpet. And he asked all of 'our' children and teachers to leave. Immediately. In the rain. I was livid and couldn't help shouting at him, 'You will be accountable for this on the Day of Judgement.' He responded calmly by saying he would put it all in writing.

My neighbour Alison suggested the *madrasa* might be more welcome at a nearby college where she was teaching foreign-language students. We went to have a look: classes could now be held in individual rooms with electronic whiteboards, and we could use the dance hall for prayers.

We moved. Everything happens for a reason.

What were they learning?

My mother still harboured some concerns. 'What do they learn in the *madrasas*?' she asked me. 'I've seen them rock backwards and forwards on television.'

Like all *madrasas*, we taught Qur'an reading and pronunciation, Islamic rituals and Islamic character. But we also wanted the children to learn about their belief in God, the signs of His creation, and stories of the many prophets, while having fun at the same time.

The children saw how flowers took in water through their stems and tried to part the water in a Tupperware container to see for themselves what a difficult job Moses had facing the Red Sea. The children discovered the miracle of the water cycle and together sponsored an orphan from overseas. When it was the *madrasa Eid* party, they played 'pin the door on the Kaa'ba' and wrestled with 'Pass the Parcel' – with questions on Islam stuck in–between the wrappers. When it was Mothers Day, they learnt about the emphasis on all mothers in Islam. And they had an opportunity once a week to develop friendships with other Muslims in an environment not too dissimilar from school.

After the older children learnt about a Prophet called Shuaib, who taught the merchants and traders around him to transact honestly with their customers, an external speaker came in to the *madrasa* to run a 'fair-trade' business game. The children had to consider the ethical principles behind buying products from the developing world, and discussed how it was sometimes fairer to pay more. The *madrasa* also held an open morning during fair-trade fortnight, for Fitra mothers and other mothers in the area to talk over fair-trade coffee and biscuits. My Diwali-loving neighbour Jane came along and ended up chatting to my friend and co-teacher Allia. When Jane and I subsequently met at the church playgroup, she revealed what they had been talking about. 'We were discussing leg-waxing, it was hilarious,' Jane said, tickled that anyone wearing all that black would have an opinion about how to deal with hairy legs.

We were here first

As I was teaching maths at a nearby mixed state secondary school, I saw how important it was for children as well as adults from different backgrounds to find out more about each other.

One Friday afternoon, a 14-year old girl appeared very distressed: a couple of boys had ripped off her *hijab* in the lunch-hour. She was feeling violated and embarrassed. The following week, the head of Religious Education sat the offending boys down for a chat and – since she had just bumped into me by the photocopier an hour earlier – she asked me to join her.

The head of RE asked the boys why they did it. They just shrugged. One said: 'I didn't think it was a big deal, Miss.' She asked them how they would feel if someone pulled down their trousers. 'Oh, I wouldn't mind, Miss, after all, we are all the same down there aren't we?' came the unexpected response. The boys were 15; the teacher firmly clarified that we were not all the same. I explained that the girl wore the scarf for modesty and that this girl would have felt as bad as if they had pulled down her skirt. The boys were shocked: 'I had no idea, Miss,' said one.

The teacher then asked how many girls they thought there were in the school who wore the scarf. After a pause, one of the lads said: 'I think about 600.' This boy badly needed some maths lessons: there were only 1,500 pupils in the school, of whom around half were girls, of whom around 15 were Muslim – and a handful wore a scarf. I found it interesting that the boy had imagined scarf-wearing girls dominated the school. He went onto complain: 'These Muslims walk about in groups with knives. And they all live together in the same area of town, so that we will think they own the place. But we were here first.'

The teacher told them what it was like to enter the local supermarket being a minority. She was also a minority in Woking: she was black. And she felt people were staring at her. 'It is not easy looking different, you know,' she told them, hoping they might start to empathize. I added that most of the Muslim girls – and the boys in the school were as British as anyone else: they were born in the UK and had lived in England all their lives. The boys were genuinely intrigued by the information they had been given and promised it would not happen again.

A week later, I passed one of the teenagers in the corridor. He rushed up to me. 'Thanks so much for the lesson the other day, Miss,

I really learnt a lot. See you, Miss.' And off he ran. Initially I couldn't remember where and what I had taught him. Which maths group was he in? What lesson had he learned? And then I remembered. I was amazed and impressed by his new positive attitude. One day, I hoped he might even pass it on to his own children.

All change

And then everything changed. Julian came home from work and told me he had been offered an opportunity in South Africa that was too good for us all to turn down. We were going to have to leave our community, our family, and our home. I was going to have to stop teaching at the secondary school. Our three children were going to have to leave their school, their nurseries and their *madrasa*. I felt sick.

I had been living in England since birth, apart from a couple of very temporary stays abroad as a young child. I didn't have another home – and nor did my children. I couldn't imagine living anywhere else. England was organized, the Muslims were diverse and, compared to South Africa, the country was so safe. In the chaos that was family life, I often left the keys in the lock in the front door. No one ever walked in – apart from Julian. I was going to have to learn to be much more careful. In South Africa, concerns about security were very real – and the concerns were very local. The most likely place for an attack was going to be my driveway.

Leaving home

My local community helped me to leave.

Bethany Babes arranged ice creams on the church lawn to say goodbye to Asim and Amaani. I met up with Lena, Rachel, Claire and Wendy in the forest nearby, so that our collection of children could race around the woods together for the last time. My next-door neighbour Barbara accompanied the children and me to the numerous vaccinations we were recommended to have, assisting with calming the progressively loud screams that emanated from the doctor's surgery. Saji, my ex-Sikh Malaysian friend, came by and dropped off delicious home-cooked food.

Nasheeba went through all my different lists, making sure that in between getting a new safety-compliant door for the boiler for prospective tenants, applying for visas, and returning all the children's books to the library, I had remembered to get the girls some wedding socks and smart hairclips. She knew that immediately after our house was due to be packed up, I was travelling to a close family wedding: the wedding of Julian's brother Daniele to a warm-hearted and quietly intelligent Canadian, Kathryn, who had recently converted to Islam. Daniele had realized that marriage didn't mean leaving the family, after all. Nasheeba encouraged me to stay calm in the midst of my lists, and to ask God for help. I needed it.

Susie, my neighbour and school run partner, promised she would make sure that all the children's school uniform and ballet outfits would find good homes. Farah, from the Fitra *madrasa* committee, looked after my youngest children for many afternoons – and had to put up with Amaani unsuccessfully attempting to toilet-train herself in the back garden. Helen, with whom I enjoyed the trip to the beach, invited the children and me over for afternoon tea. Rahat, also heavily involved in Fitra, helped me to sort out which things from around the house needed to go to charity and which things should be sent for recycling. Neighbours Pauline, Jane and Alison held a 'last supper' for us and all of our children to interact over Spaghetti Bolognese and yet more cups of tea. And Sofia, Danyal's mother, coordinated a leaving party. No one wore a hat.

And then I said goodbye to all the children at the *madrasa*. I thought it would be a good time to remind them about their identity, and what their Fitra was all about. As the 70 children between the ages of three and 17 sat in front of me, I asked the children what religion they were. 'Muslim' they all shouted, albeit not in unison. I asked the children where they were from. There were a few shouts of 'Egypt', 'Syria,' 'Pakistan,' 'Iraq'. Safiyya and Asim, along with the majority of the children there, shouted out at the tops of their voices: 'England'.

My youngest child Amaani, now aged three, put her hand up – she was sitting at the front. I bent down and asked her gently: 'And where are you from, Amaani?' I hoped her identity would already be as solid as everybody else's at the *madrasa*. But, in fact, it was much more flexible.

'I'm from South Africa,' Amaani announced, with a cheeky grin on her face.

Epilogue

In South Africa, as in England, Christmas is approaching once again. Asim, age five – and who is now learning to read both 'forwards' and 'backwards' – has unsuccessfully attempted to withdraw himself from the school carol service. He says there is not enough about *Eid* in it. In contrast, nine-year-old Safiyya is dancing around the house, practising the words for one of her songs.

'So many people livin' in fear, please hear our prayer and stop all the killing,
Let this be the Christmas, let this be the year.
Give me an African Christmas, peace and love to heal our land
We need an African Christmas, spending together, hand in hand.'

Amen to that.

Polly, the family friend who suffered from severe burns and who lost her husband Dan in the Bali bombings, has emailed me from England. The 'Dan's Fund for Burns' that she set up is doing well: nearly a million pounds has been raised for burns survivors in England and other parts of the UK. Many of them are Muslim – and many of them are not. It looks like some good did come out of the bombings after all.

And I now have an alternative answer for the little boy in England who wanted to know about Muslim children, who asked me: 'What is the weather like in their world?' I can tell you that for those children living in 'our world' it is almost permanently sunny.

Even though I don't miss the weather, I do miss the country I call home. But I will still be English – whenever I am in the world. And, God willing, I will also be a Muslim. My neighbour Helen remains ever hopeful that I may change.

Glossary of Arabic Terms

Abaya: Full length cloak, usually black.

Adhan: The call to prayer for Muslims, made five times a day. It is also whispered into the ears of newborn babies.

Alhamdulillah: Commonly used expression, meaning 'Praise be to God'. It is said as a response, for example after being asked 'How are you?'

Allah: Arabic name for the One God, similar to the word used by Jews in Hebrew and by early Christians in Aramaic. Allah is the same God worshipped by Christians and Jews.

Allahu Akbar: God is the Greatest.

Assalamu Alaikum: Muslim greeting meaning 'Peace be upon you'.

Bismillah: Commonly used expression, meaning 'In the name of God'. It is said before starting any activity, for example before eating.

Dua: Literally, calling. Refers to invocations, supplications and prayers to God.

Eid ul Adha: Festival celebrated near the end of *Hajj*, to commemorate Abraham's willingness to sacrifice his son for God.

Eid ul Fitr: Festival celebrating the end of the holy month of *Ramadan* during which Muslims fast.

Eid: Literally, festival.

Fatwa: Legal opinion.

Fiqh: Understanding of Islamic law.

Fitra: Innate God-consciousness; childhood innocence.

Gibreel: Arabic for Gabriel.

Hadith: Literally, speech. Refers to the record of what Muhammad said, did, or tacitly approved.

Hajj: The annual pilgrimage to Mecca which Muslims must undertake once in their lifetime; one of the five pillars of Islam. The timing of the annual *Hajj* is fixed according to the lunar calendar.

Hajji: A person who is currently on *Hajj*, or who has already been on *Hajj*.

Halal: Anything permissible under Islamic law. This includes behaviour, speech, dress, conduct, manner, dietary laws. Opposite of *haram*.

Haram: That which is forbidden. This includes behaviour, speech, dress, conduct, manner, dietary laws. Opposite of *halal*.

Hijab: Literally, to cover. Often refers to the headscarf worn by Muslim women but encompasses the principle of modesty, including dress and behaviour.

Iftar: Literally, 'breakfast'. Meal served at the end of the day during the holy month of Ramadan, to break the day's fast.

Ihram: A sacred state into which Muslim must enter into when performing *Hajj* or *Umrah*.

Imam: Literally, leader. Refers to the political leader of the state, historically, or a religious leader, or the leader of congregational prayers.

Insha'Allah: Commonly used expression, meaning 'God willing'.

Isa: Arabic name for Jesus.

Jihad: Literally, exerting or striving. Refers to exerting oneself in striving towards perfection in control of oneself, doing good deeds and abstaining from evil ones. Also used to refer to sacrifice of one's wealth, physical effort and life in defence of one's life, family, property or faith.

Jummah: Congregational prayers, obligatory for men, performed on a Friday and preceded by a sermon.

Ka'bah: The holiest and most sacred building in Islam located in Mecca. Muslims pray facing in this direction.

Lailat ul Qadr: Literally, Night of Power. Marks the anniversary of the night on which Muhammad first began receiving revelations from God through the Angel Gabriel. Occurs during the month of Ramadan.

Madrasa: Literally, school. Now refers to place of learning about Islam for Muslim schoolchildren, usually after school.

Mahr: A mandatory gift in Islam, given by the groom to the bride upon marriage.

Mihrab: A niche in the wall of a mosque that indicates the direction of *Ka'bah* that Muslims should face when praying.

Minbar: A pulpit in the mosque where the *Imam* stands to deliver sermons.

Muslim: Literally, one who submits. Now means one who believes in one God and that Muhammad is the final prophet of God.

Nikah: Literally, contract. An Arabic term for marriage.

Niqab: A veil that covers the face, worn by some Muslim women as part of their *hijab*.

Qur'an: Literally, recitation. The sacred text of Islam revealed to Muhammad.

Raka'ah: One unit of set actions of Islamic prayer. The shortest obligatory prayer consists of two *raka'ah*.

Ramadan: The month of obligatory fasting. The ninth month of the Islamic calendar.

Salah: The ritual prayer practised by Muslims in supplication to God.

Shahadah: From the verb 'to testify'. The Muslim declaration of faith in the Oneness of God and in Muhammad as His final prophet.

Sharia: Literally, path. The code of law derived from the *Qur'an* and the teachings and example of Muhammad. *Sharia* is only applicable to Muslims.

Surah: Chapter of the *Qur'an*.

Sujud: Prostration before God. In this position, the nose and forehead touch the ground.

Tarawih: Additional optional evening prayers, performed during *Ramadan*.

Taqwa: Awareness of God. Specifically, following the commands of

God and avoiding His prohibitions, both outwardly and inwardly, with a sense of the glorification, reverence, awe and fear of God.

Tawaf: The ritual of walking around the Ka'bah seven times.

Thobe: A long shirtlike dress worn by Arab men. Usually made of white cotton.

Ummah: Literally, group, community or nation. Used in the *Qur'an* to refer to different groups or nations and also specifically to the universal Muslim community.

Umrah: Optional Muslim pilgrimage to Mecca that can be performed any time of the year.

Wali: Representative or guardian. Specifically refers to a person representing the bride's welfare at the time of the marriage ceremony, or *Nikah*.

Wudu: The act of washing parts of the body in a prescribed way using water. Muslims are required to perform *wudu* in preparation for the five daily prayers.

Zabihah: An animal slaughtered according to the Islamic method.

Zakah: 2.5 per cent of wealth given yearly. One of the five pillars of Islam.

Notes

A note on *hadiths*. Each saying of Muhammad has two parts to it: the text of the *hadith* and the names of those who heard it and related it to others. Only the first person in the chain of narration has been mentioned in these references. The sayings have been compiled into collections of *hadiths* reported by Muslim scholars such as al-Bukhari within a few hundred years of Muhammad's death; they are well known to Muslims throughout the world. The major collections have been subsequently translated from Arabic to English.

Introduction

1. http://www.statistics.gov.uk/cci/nugget.asp?id=463, accessed 10 August 2007.
2. YouGov Survey, *Attitudes Towards British Muslims*. Report commissioned by Islamic Society of Britain, 2002, http://www.isb.org.uk/iaw/docs/SurveyIAW2002.pdf. (Not formally published but reported in the media.)
3. USA Today/Gallup Poll, 28–30 July 2006, http://www.gallup.com/poll/24073/AntiMuslim-Sentiments-Fairly-Commonplace.aspx.
4. Dorling D. and Thomas B. (2004), *People and Places: A 2001 Census Atlas of the UK.* Polity Press.
5. Dorling D. (2005), Why Trevor is wrong about race ghettoes, *Observer,* 25 September.

Chapter 1: Embracing Faith

1. *Hadith* recorded in al-Bukhari.
2. Rushdie, S. (1988), *The Satanic Verses,* Viking, pp. 91, 114, 123.
3. Haneef, S. (1986), *What Everyone Should Know about Islam and Muslims,* Kazi Publications.
4. Shanks, H. (1993), *Understanding the Dead Sea Scrolls,* Random House; Harpur, T. (1993), *For Christ's Sake,* McClellan & Stewart, p. xii.
5. The only verse in the Qur'an mentioning four wives is in the context of orphans, in 4:3. In Lang, J. (1994), *Struggling to Surrender,* Amana Publications, p. 163, Jeffery Lang interprets the verse to mean that marrying the widows and older female orphans was allowed in order to protect the orphans – both boys and girls.
6. Monty Python (1979), *Life of Brian,* Handmade Films.
7. Alkhuli, M.A. (1987), *The Need for Islam,* International Islamic Publishing House.
8. Miller, W. (1986), *A Christian's Response to Islam,* Kingsway.
9. Sarwar, G. (1982), *Islam: Belief and Teachings,* Muslim Educational Trust.
10. Hamid, A.W. (1989), *Islam the Natural Way,* MELS Publishing.
11. It is reported in a *hadith* that Muhammad said: 'It is (to offer the best) for a day and a night, and hospitality extends for three days. What is beyond that is charity.' Recorded in al-Bukhari.
12. Hijab, N. (1989), *Womanpower: the Arab Debate on Women at Work,* Cambridge University Press.
13. Mernissi, F. (1985), *Beyond the Veil: Male-Female Dynamics in Muslim Society,* Al Saqi Books.
14. It is reported in a *hadith* that Angel Gabriel asked Muhammad: 'What is *ihsan*?' He answered: '*Ihsan* is to worship God as though you see him. And if you do not see him, surely He sees you.' Recorded in al-Bukhari.
15. A clear book has subsequently been written on this subject. Al-Toma, B. (2002), *A Simple Guide to Prayer,* The Islamic Foundation and Islamia Media.
16. It is reported in a *hadith* that Muhammad said: '*Dua* is the essence of worship.' Recorded in at-Tirmidhi.

Chapter 2: Marriage Ties and Scarves

1. It is reported in a *hadith* that 'Umar ibn al-Khattab said that Muhammad said: "A man and woman do not remain alone in privacy except that the third among them Shaytan."' Recorded in at-Tirmidhi.

2. *Census April 2001,* Office for National Statistics.

3. Self, A. and Zealey, L. (2007), *Social Trends 37,* Office for National Statistics.

4. It is reported in a *hadith* that Muhammad said: 'There is no *nikah* except with a *wali*.' Recorded in at-Tirmidhi.

5. 'And give unto women their dowry in the spirit of a gift; but if they, of their own accord, give up unto you aught thereof, then enjoy it with pleasure and good cheer.' Qur'an 4:4.

6. Asad, M. (1980), *Meaning of the Qur'an,* New Era Publications.

7. As specified by the UK Deed Poll Service, www.ukdps.co.uk.

8. Boxer, D. (2006), *All Things Considered,* 13 June, NPR.

9. This ended with the 1882 Married Property Act.

10. It is reported in a *hadith* that Muhammad said: 'Whoever believes in God and the Last Day, let him not sit at a table where wine is being served.' Recorded in at-Tirmidhi.

11. *Hadith* recorded in al-Muwatta. Story also relayed in www.mkgandhi-sarvodaya.org/humantouch.htm, accessed 15 May 2007.

12. legs and body shape ... It is reported in a *hadith* that 'Aisha, daughter of Abu Bakr, entered upon the house of Muhammad wearing thin clothes. Muhammad turned his attention from her. He said: "O Asma', when a woman reaches the age of menstruation, it does not suit her that she displays her parts of the body except this and this," and he pointed to her face and hands.' Recorded in Abu Dawud.

13. Moir, A. and Jessel, D. (1991), *Brainsex: The Real Difference between Men and Women,* Mandarin.

14. Bercot, D. *The Christian Woman's Head Covering Through the Centuries* www.scrollpublishing.com/store/head-covering-history.html, accessed 30 May 2007.

15. It is reported in a *hadith* that Muhammad took some silk in his right hand and some gold in his left hand and then he said, 'These two are *haram* for the males among my followers.' Recorded in at-Tirmidhi.

16. Hamid, A.W. (1989), *Islam the Natural Way*, MELS Publishing, pp. 85–87.

Chapter 3: On Foreign Soil

1. Stranger or a traveller ... *Hadith* reported in al-Bukhari.

2. It is reported in a *hadith* that Abu Sa'eed al-Khudri said: 'While Muhammad was leading his companions in prayer, he took off his shoes and placed them to his left. When the people saw that, they took off their shoes too. When Muhammad finished his prayer, he asked, "What made you take off your shoes?" They said, "We saw you take off your shoes, so we took ours off too." Muhammad said "Angel Gabriel came to me and told me that there was something dirty on them."' Recorded in Abu Dawood.

3. It is reported in a *hadith* that Muhammad asked: 'Is any of you incapable of reciting a third of the Qur'an in a night?' and then proceeded to instruct: 'Recite *Sura al-Ikhlas*, for (by the One in whose hands is my life), it is equivalent to (reading) a third of the Qur'an.' Recorded in al-Bukhari.

4. 'For I neither received it from man, neither was I taught (it), but by the revelation of Jesus Christ.' Galatians 1:12

5. Acts 9:3–20

6. Myre, G. (2006), For West Bank, it's a highway to frustration, *New York Times*, 18 November 2006.

7. Office for the Co-ordination of Humanitarian Affairs (2007), *The Humanitarian Impact on Palestinians of Israeli Settlements and Other Infrastructure in the West Bank*, United Nations.

8. Luke 4:1–13.

9. For example, in a hadith reported by Anas bin Malik. Recorded in al-Bukhari.

10. Asad, M. (1980), *Meaning of the Qur'an*, New Era Publications, pp. 996–8.

11. Lings, M. (1988), *Muhammad: His Life Based on the Earliest Sources*, Unwin Paperbacks, pp. 29–30, p. 44.

12. 'But as soon as the two had tasted (the fruit) of the tree, they became conscious of their nakedness; and they began to cover themselves with pieced-together leaves from the garden.' Qur'an 7:21.

Chapter 4: In the 'Real World'

1. Lings, M. (1988), *Muhammad: His Life Based on the Earliest Sources,* Unwin Paperbacks, pp. 34–5.
2. Khattab H., (1993), *The Muslim Woman's Handbook,* Ta Ha Publishers, pp. 31–2.
3. Ahmed, A.S. (1992), *Postmodernism and Islam: Predicament and Promise,* Routledge.
4. It is reported in a *hadith* that Aishah said: 'Muhammad used to sew his clothes, mend his sandals, and do what other men do in their homes.' Recorded in Ahmad.
5. It is reported in a *hadith* that Muhammad said: 'A woman whom has been previously married has more right concerning herself than her guardian, and a virgin's consent must be asked about herself.' Recorded in al-Bukhari.
6. It is reported in a *hadith* that Ibn Abbas said Muhammad said: 'The One who made drinking it *haram* has made selling it *haram*.' Recorded in al-Muwatta.
7. It is reported in a *hadith* that Aishah said Muhammad said: 'Verily the one who recites the Qur'an beautifully, smoothly, and precisely, he will be in the company of the noble and obedient angels. And as for the one who recites with difficulty, stammering or stumbling through its verses, then he will have twice that reward.' Recorded in al-Bukhari.

Chapter 5: A Pilgrim's Progress

1. *Hadith* recorded in at-Tirmidhi.
2. It is reported in a *hadith* that Muhammad said: 'A man who decides to perform Hajj should act with promptness, for he may fall sick, or his mount may get lost, or a need may arise that becomes an obstacle.' Recorded in Ibn Majah.
3. It is reported in a *hadith* that Muhammad said: 'He who performs Hajj for Allah and does not behave in an obscene manner or acts unlawfully, will return sinless as in the day he was born.' Recorded in al-Bukhari and Muslim.

4. Keller N.H.M. (1994), *Reliance of the Traveller*, Sunna Books, pp. 312–20.

5. *Hadith* recorded in Muslim.

6. *Hadith* recorded in at-Tirmidhi.

7. *Hadith* recorded in Ahmad and at-Tirmidhi.

8. Emerick, Y. (1999), *What Islam is All About*, International Books and Tapes Supply, pp. 315–16.

9. Jeenah, N. and Shaikh, S. (2000), *Journey of Discovery: A South African Hajj*, Full Moon Press, pp. 69–70.

10. Peters, F.E. (1994), *A Reader on Classical Islam*, Princeton University Press. pp. 3–41.

11. Reported by the Islamic Cultural Centre. *http://iccuk.org/media/reports/about_25000_british_muslims_to_perform_Hajj_this_year.htm*, accessed 5 July 2007.

Chapter 6: Babes in Arms

1. *Hadith* recorded in al-Bukhari and Muslim.

2. *Hadith* collected by Ibn Hajar al-Asqalaanee.

3. Global Strategy for Infant and Young Child Feeding, http://www.who.int/nutrition/publications/gs_infant_feeding_text_eng.pdf.

4. Shaykh al-Islam Ibn Taymiyah, *Al-Ikhtiyaaraat al-Fiqhiyyah min Fataawa*, p. 246.

5. *Hadith* related by at-Tabaraanee.

6. Simon, B. (2001), *60 Minutes*, CBS 19 August.

7. Sardar, Z. and Davies, M.W. (2004), *The No-Nonsense Guide to Islam:* Verso, pp. 60–3.

8. Al-Areefee, Y.I.A. (1996), *Manners of Welcoming the New Born Child in Islaam*, Maktaba Dar-us-Salam, pp. 30–4.

9. *ibid*. pp. 35–7.

10. It is related in a *hadith* that Abu Musa said: 'I had a new-born baby; I took him to Muhammad, who called him Ibrahim. Muhammad chewed a date then he took it and rubbed the inside of the baby's mouth with it and supplicated for blessings for him and handed him to me.' Recorded in al-Bukhari.

11. Al-Areefee, Y.I.A. (1996), op. cit. pp. 76–84.

12. *ibid.* pp. 52–75.
13. *ibid.* pp. 85-94.
14. Gillan, G. (2003), Algerian pilot sues over terror charges, *Guardian,* 16 September 2003.
15. Ramadan, T. (2005), *For a Moratorium on the Application of Sharia in the Muslim World* : Le Monde. 4 April 2005.

Chapter 7: Community Spirit

1. *Hadith* recorded in Tahhawi.
2. It is related in a *hadith* by Jabir that Muhammad said: 'For me the earth has been made a mosque and a means of purification; therefore, if prayer overtakes any person of my community, he should say his prayers (wherever he is …).' Recorded in al-Bukhari.
3. Abu Hanifa said: 'Do not write down everything you hear from me, for it happens that I hold one opinion today and reject it tomorrow, or hold one opinion tomorrow and reject it the day after tomorrow.' Shaikh Al-Albaani, N. (1993) *The Prophet's Prayer Described from the Beginning to End as Though You See It,* Al Haneef Publications, p. ix.
4. It is related in a *hadith* that Muhammad said this when his daughter Umm Kulthum was laid on her grave. Reported by Abu Hanifah and Ahmad.
5. Iraq's potential cachet of weapons has been documented, among others, by the James Martin Centre for Non-Proliferation Studies in the US, www.cns.miis.edu/research/wmdme/iraq.htm.
6. Blix, H., Oral introduction to the twelfth quarterly report of UNMOVIC to the UN Security Council, 7 March 2003, http://www.un.org/apps/news/ infocusnewsiraq.asp?NewsID=414&sID=6.
7. The Claremont Institute in the US has documented details of the Russian Topol-M missile and its testing programme, www.missilethreat.com/ missilesoftheworld/id.145/missile_detail.asp.
8. Also documented by US Government Energy Information Administration, www.eia.doe.gov.
9. Sardar, Z. and Davies, M.W. (2004), *The No-nonsense Guide to Islam,* New Internationalist Publication Ltd.

10. Ali, Y.A. (1975), *The Holy Qur'an: text, translation and commentary,* The Islamic Foundation.

11. Esposito, J.L. (2005), *Islam: The Straight Path,* Oxford University Press, p. 93.

12. *The logic of suicide terrorism,* American Conservative, 18 July 2005; Pape, R. (2005) *Dying to Win: The Strategic Logic of Suicide Terrorism,* Random House.

Chapter 8: Fasting and Feasting

1. *Hadith* recorded in at-Tirmidhi.

2. Sheikh al-Hilaalee, S. and Sheikh Abdul-Hameed, A.H.A. (1995), *Fasting in Ramadaan as Observed by the Prophet,* Al-Hidaayah Publishing and Distribution.

3. *Hadith* recorded in Darimi.

4. *Hadith* recorded in Ibn Majah and Ahmad.

5. *Fatwa* 2769 issued by the Council of Senior Scholars in the Kingdom of Saudi Arabia.

6. It is related in a *hadith* that Muhammad said: 'Seven (types of) people will be covered with God's shade on a day when there is no shade but His Shade, (from among them) a man who gives a charity hiding it, that (even) his left hand does not know what his right hand has spent.' Recorded in al-Bukhari; see also the Bible – Matthew 6:3.

7. It is related in a *hadith* that Muhammad said: 'Whoever does not give up false speech and false actions and ignorance, God has no need of his giving up his food and drink.' Recorded in al-Bukhari.

8. Sheikh al-Hilaalee, S. and Sheikh Abdul-Hameed, A.H.A. (1995), *op.cit.* pp. 82–7.

9. Reid, R.H. (2004), A fine balance, *Guardian,* 10 November 2004.

10. See the poem by Hamod, S. (2004), *This night in Fallujah: Lailat Al Qadr in Ramadan.* 6 November 2004, www.counterpunch.org/poems11082004.html, accessed 15 September 2007.

Chapter 9: The Next Generation

1. *Hadith* recorded by al-Tirmidhi.
2. Islamia Schools Trust (1989), *Islamic Teachings Course,* Volume 2.
3. 'And the swine, because it divideth the hoof, yet cheweth not the cud, it is unclean unto you: ye shall not eat of their flesh, nor touch their dead carcasses.' (Deuteronomy 14:8).
4. 'And their boast, "Behold, we have slain the Christ Jesus, son of Mary, (who claimed to be) the Apostle of God!" However, they did not slay him, neither did they crucify him, but it only seemed to them (as if it had been so) ... ' Qur'an 4:157
5. DfES (2003) *Aiming High: Raising the Achievement of Minority Ethnic Pupils*. DfES.
6. Parker-Jenkins, M. (1995), *Children of Islam: A Teacher's Guide to Meeting the Needs of Muslim Pupils,* Trentham Books Ltd.
7. *ibid.* pp. 59–82.
8. It is reported in a hadith that Muhammad said: 'To purify (cleanse) the utensils belonging to one of you, if it has been licked by a dog, wash it seven times, using soil the first time.' Recorded in Muslim. It is reported in another *hadith* that the dogs came into and went out of the mosque in the time of Muhammad, and they did not wash (the mosque) with water on that account. Recorded in al-Bukhari.